D0111409

TWO HUNDRED

TRADITIONAL TYPES

ITALIAN
CHEESE

A guide to their discovery and appreciation

Slow Food Editore

edited by
Piero Sardo, Gigi Piumatti,
Roberto Rubino

texts
Piero Sardo, Armando Gambera,
Cinzia Scaffidi, Vincenzo Ferrara,
Enrico Surra

collaborators
Enrico Azzolin, Gino Bortoletto,
Pier Bottà, Michele Bruno,
Dionisio Castello, Angelo Concas,
Luca Fabbri, Nadia Innocente,
Clara Laurita, Giuseppe Licitra,
Nereo Pederzolli, Michele Pizzillo,
Carmine Ragusa

editorial committee
Marcello Marengo, Bianca Minerdo,
Gigi Piumatti, Cinzia Scaffidi

co-ordinating editor
Maria Vittoria Negro

translation editor
Giles Watson

translations
Helen Donald, Michael Farrell,
Giles Watson

art director
Dante Albieri

graphic design
Stefano Pallaro

layout
Maurizio Burdese, Davide Gandino,
Francesco Perona

photographs
Tino Gerbaldo - Bra

cover
Photograph by Fernando Zanetti

offset litho
Ponti - Boves

printed by
Centro Stampa Srl- Bra (Cuneo)

Slow Food Arcigola Editore srl
Via della Mendicità Istruita, 45
12042 Bra (Cuneo)
tel.+39 0172 419611
fax +39 0172 411218

for advertising enquiries contact
Slow Food Arcigola Promozione
Roberto Burdese, Ivan Piasentin
tel.+39 0172 419611
fax +39 0172 421293

E-mail: info@slowfood.com
Website: www.slowfood.com

ISBN: 88-86283-98-9

We wish to thank the following companies and organisations for kindly supplying cheeses

Abruzzo and Molise
Esperya, Loreto (Ancona)
Taberna Imperiale, Silvi Marina (Teramo)

Basilicata
ANFOSC, Bella (Potenza)
Istituto Sperimentale per la Zootecnia, Bella (Potenza)

Calabria
Agenzia Regionale per lo Sviluppo e i Servizi in Agricoltura, Cosenza

Campania
Antonello Di Masi, Albanella (Salerno)
La Baronia, Pontelatone (Caserta)
Madaio, Eboli (Salerno)

Emilia Romagna
Amerigo dal 1934, Savigno (Bologna)

Friuli-Venezia Giulia
Malga Rio Secco di Maria Carmen Buzzi Spironelli, Pontebba (Udine)
Latterie Friulane, Campoformido (Udine)

Lazio
Cooperativa Produttori Cisterna Cisterna di Latina (Latina)
La Tradizione, Rome
Pane e Vino, Frosinone

Liguria
Cooperativa Casearia Val di Vara Varese Ligure (La Spezia)
La Bottega di Angela Maria Molini di Triora (Imola)

Lombardy
Consorzio di Tutela Bitto e Valtellina Casera, Sondrio
Ganassa, Ballabio (Lecco)
Guffanti, Arona (Novara)
Ol Formager, Bergamo

Marche
Caseificio La Ripa, Orciano di Pesaro (Pesaro)
Esperya, Loreto (Ancona)

Piedmont
Agrinatura Occelli, Farigliano (Cuneo)
Arbiora, Cessole (Asti)
Casa del Formaggio, Saluzzo (Cuneo)
Il Cornale, Magliano Alfieri, (Cuneo)
Cedis Bra (Cuneo)

Giolito Formaggi, Bra (Cuneo)
Guffanti, Arona (Novara)
Stagionatura Valcasotto, Pamparato (Cuneo)

Puglia
Caseificio Tarantino, Gravina (Bari)
Taberna Imperiale, Silvi Marina (Teramo)

Sardinia
Bonu Formaggi, Cagliari
Cisalpino, Savigliano (Cuneo)
Ente Regionale di Sviluppo e Assistenza Tecnica in Agricoltura, Cagliari
I Sapori della Tradizione, Cagliari

Sicily
Assessorato Regionale Agricoltura e Foreste Sezione Operativa N°. 8
Sant'Agata di Militello (Messina)
Assessorato Regionale Agricoltura e Foreste Sezione Operativa N°. 29
Palazzolo Acreide (Siracusa)
Assessorato Regionale Agricoltura e Foreste Sezione Operativa N°. 59, Mezzojuso (Palermo)
Consorzio di Ricerca Filiera Lattiero-Casearia, Ragusa
Taberna Imperiale, Silvi Marina (Teramo)

Tuscany
Il Forteto, Vicchio di Mugello (Florence)
San Polo, Pienza (Siena)
Vecchio Mulino Castelnuovo Garfagnana (Lucca)
Zummo Formaggi, Pistoia

Trentino-Alto Adige
Consorzio Trentingrana-Concast, Trento
Taberna Imperiale, Silvi Marina (Teramo)

Umbria
Il Bacco Felice, Foligno (Perugia)

Valle d'Aosta
Assessorato Agricoltura e Risorse Naturali Direzione Assistenza Tecnica, Quart (Aosta)

Veneto
Caseificio Roncolato, Roncà (Verona)
La Casearia di Carpenedo, Povegliano (Treviso)

A heritage halved

This book describes and documents with original texts and photographs two hundred and one traditional cheeses. That's an impressive figure. But tracking down information and cheeses to photograph has been no easy task. Haven't experts always maintained that there are more than four hundred cheeses in Italy? This is in fact confirmed by the 1991 edition of the *Atlante dei prodotti tipici: i formaggi* ("Atlas of Typical Products – Cheeses"), compiled for INSOR by Corrado Barberis and Graziella Picchi. The volume, still indispensable for anyone exploring Italy's cheesemaking heritage and, indeed, our own source of inspiration, lists exactly four hundred and three types. Is it possible that the number has halved in eight years? We think not, even though standardisation has for some years been causing a steady reduction in small-scale local cheesemaking

The remaining cheeses are the result of a harsh process of natural selection in that, over the centuries, only the finest cheeses have survived. These are the ones that add most value to the livestock farmed in their particular territory. Yet when the global market began to alter consumer perceptions, the long-triumphant products of centuries-old skills went into decline. Generally speaking, traditional cheeses are made in mountainous or outlying areas by individual families producing small quantities, often in conditions that may not be scrupulously germ-free. In contrast, globalisation demands large quantities, competitive prices, a continuous production cycle and guaranteed hygiene so, in practice, EC legislation has enshrined the interests of food multinationals in community law. Consumers have been willing accomplices. They have betrayed local products for the siren song of the hypermarket's refrigerated counter. The cheeses people buy in such outlets are sanitised, odourless and made from pasteurised milk by machines that spit them out as if they were die-cast. If this book had taken industrially produced cheeses into consideration, we would have gone well beyond four hundred types. But we had other ends in mind. We were not drawing up an inventory of Italy's cheeses. Our objective was to rescue what still survives of the country's cheesemaking tradition. Today, that heritage comprises the two hundred and one cheeses you will find in this book, and some – not very many – others that we have not included because they differed only in name or shape from the ones listed here. One or two we were simply unable to include. These "untouchables" include cheeses that are produced by a single cheesemaker who has no desire to market them more widely, seasonal cheeses, and types whose characteristics have been altered irrevocably to adapt them to market demands.

Many other types, however, have simply disappeared in recent years. For decades, it has been impossible to obtain Montebore dei Colli Tortonesi, a cheese frequently mentioned in the literature, or Solandro Trentino, Slattato Marchigiano, Granone di Lodi, Caprino del Fara from Lazio, Campania's Cacio Peruto, Caprino di Farindola from Molise or Basilicata's Pecorino di Zaccuni or Padraccio. Marciano has disappeared from Calabria. Calcagno is only a memory in Sicily. And so the list goes on. The cries for help coming from farmhouse cheesemakers, especially in the South, are ominous. Small-scale producers have great difficulty in marketing their cheeses for there are simply no appropriate outlets. While the Salone del Gusto in Turin showed that demand for high quality cheese exists and is far from being a market niche, these products still find it extremely difficult to acquire visibility, accessibility and consumer appeal. You can't make a living out of the Salone del Gusto alone. Consumers have to be informed and prompted to make choices that overcome the temptation to take the line of least resistance. If only they looked, ordinary cheeselovers may even find they have, only a few kilometres from home, a farmer who makes a fine ewe's milk cheese, for example. Round the corner, there could be a serious delicatessen. In fact, the maître at their favourite restaurant may only be waiting for an excuse to provide a decent cheeseboard. "Never say die", is the watchword.

However, it is legitimate to ask, "Is it worth going to these lengths?", especially when you end up spending more. We believe it is. Compare an industrial cheese with one skilfully made using unpasteurised milk from local cows. The "taste gap" is immediately apparent, even to an inexperienced palate. All consumers have to do is pay a little more attention to what they are eating and they will soon realise that there is a world of difference. The industrial cheesemaker is looking to make money. The artisan wants first and foremost consumers who are knowledgeable, respectful and passionate. And whose reward will be sheer gastronomic pleasure.

Piero Sardo
Slow Food

In search of diversity

The more you explore the subject, the clearer it becomes that the variety of Italian cheeses is enormous. This is not just because Italy historically is the land of a hundred communes, and as many squabbling statelets. It is also a reflection of the country's long-suffering and extremely varied terrain. Naturally, it goes without saying that the territory of origin leaves its mark on a cheese, defining the types that can be made and their tasting characteristics. Thus the colder North offers a vast range of soft or pressed cheeses while the South has invented the *pasta filata*, or "stretched-curd", and the *cacioricotta* cooking-and-rennet-based coagulation technique to avoid climate-related conservation problems. But the wealth of Italy's heritage lies not just in the numbers of cheeses made but also in the differences within each type. A Caciocavallo Podolico made with milk from cows that have grazed on mountain pastures, which have an abundance of richly varied flora and plenty of water, will develop an attractively complex, delicate aroma. But if the animals are pastured in the sun-parched gullies of Basilicata, so dear to the novelist Carlo Levi, the cheese will have an equally distinctive, but more limited, aromatic range. Obviously, if the animals are kept indoors, the aromas will tend to be less marked. But scientific research is also showing that diet influences not just the cheese's taste characteristics but also its nutritional value. A round made with milk from animals from mountain pastures has a higher CLA (conjugate linoleic acid) content and greater antioxidant potential (calculated on the basis of antioxidant and cholesterol content) than a similar cheese made from barn-reared animals. There are also other differences for various additional factors come into play. Breed influences the structure and consistency of the interior, rennet is important for lipolysis, which gives the classic tangy flavour, and proteolysis (the classic droplets exuded by La Serena cheese, for example, are due to the vegetarian rennet used) while the natural environments used for ageing ensure the conditions necessary for the development of the desired microflora.

This guide aims to provide the "necessary conditions" to help you to select Italian cheeses but we also hope it will inspire you, once you have made your choice, to search for diversity.

Roberto Rubino
Anfosc

Contents

The thirty DOP
("Protected Designation of Origin") zones

Asiago

Bitto

Bra

Caciocavallo Silano

Canestrato Pugliese

Casciotta d'Urbino

Castelmagno

Fiore Sardo

Fontina

Formai de mut

Gorgonzola

Grana Padano

Montasio

Monte Veronese

Mozzarella di bufala Campana

Murazzano

Parmigiano Reggiano

Pecorino Romano

Pecorino Sardo

Pecorino Siciliano

Pecorino Toscano

Provolone Valpadana

Quartirolo Lombardo

Ragusano

Raschera

Robiola di Roccaverano

Taleggio

Toma Piemontese

Valle d'Aosta Fromadzo

Valtellina casera

Traditional cheesemaking

The photographs illustrate the procedures necessary to produce a **Raschera Quadrata di Alpeggio,** starting with the cutting of the soft curd. The preceding stages – the arrival of freshly drawn raw milk at the dairy, the inoculation of liquid calf's rennet, covering the container with a woollen cloth, and coagulation – are visually uninteresting.

Let's take a look. First the mass of soft curd is agitated with a fork-like *spino*. Then the whey is removed and the curd is poured into a container lined with a hemp cloth. It

is mixed vigorously by hand. Then it is knotted up in the cloth before undergoing a first manual pressing for about ten minutes on a wooden board with a draining channel. The bundle is then put into a square wooden mould and stones are placed on top to press the curd for five days. The last photograph shows the pressed curd when it has just been removed from the mould.

Obviously, the entire sequence of operations is done by hand. The cheesemaker's skill remains paramount.

It should also be noted that cheesemaking is carried out in clean and tidy, if unsophisticated, surroundings in full compliance with public health regulations. In other words, traditional production is not incompatible with hygiene.

Industrial cheesemaking

Making **Parmigiano Reggiano** is not actually an industrial process. Quite the reverse is true. Although this prestigious DOP consumes oceans of milk to produce millions of cheeses every year, production is split up among six hundred or so *caselli* – small traditional dairies – that observe the same strict standards while still managing to present significant variations on the classic "Parmesan" theme. Yet these photographs illustrating the birth of Parmigiano Reggiano are also a perfect example of standardised cheese production involving modern technology and a rigorous regime of hygiene controls. The differences with respect to craft-scale or *malga* ("mountain dairy") cheesemaking are very tangible, even though the produce does not jeopardise the product's traditional characteristics. We see the huge troughs where the cream is allowed to rise and the enormous conical vats where the milk is coagulated and the curd is processed. Two separate cheeses are made from the soft curd in each vat, and we can follow their progress in the photographs until the outer rind is stamped with an "ID", comprising the dairy number, the Consortium's symbol and the date of production. Salting is the final operation.

Maturing

Maturing begins when cold replaces warmth and damp takes over from dry in cheesemaking. Heat is the principal agent that curdles milk and separates curd from whey while lower temperatures and controlled humidity stimulate the micro-organisms and enzymes that modify the structure of the final product.

Maturing (or ageing, or curing) alters the cheese's composition, promoting the fermentation of sugars, triggering proteolysis (the breakdown of proteins) and lipolysis (the breakdown of fats). The action of microbes and enzymes completely transforms the taste characteristics of a cheese, altering its smell, taste, texture, digestibility and appearance, both inside and out. It is maturing that makes possible the extraordinary variety of cheeses. The photographs on these pages show a number of very different maturing environments. On the one hand, there are natural environments where microbes and enzymes go to work spontaneously. Cells and caves, where temperature and humidity levels are naturally suitable for ageing, are the traditionally favoured locations. Over the years, these environments acquire a unique microflora that contributes to developing the chemical and physical properties of one specific cheese. But modern technology also means it is possible to recreate maturing rooms artificially. Environmental parameters can be monitored and the cheesemaker can intervene to modify the maturing process.

From milk to table

1. Buying cheese

Let's say you want to impress your guests at a dinner party with a tempting cheeseboard. How to go about it? The first thing is that the town where you live must have a good cheese retailer. It will by now be obvious that this is not something to take for granted. The specialised outlets that were once strongholds of quality and variety are going through a very difficult period. Under pressure from large-scale retail distributors, specialist cheese shops have had to fall in line with supermarkets, where pre-packaged industrial cheese holds sway and brand names dictate consumer choice. Few retailers search out new cheeses or have any desire to explain to customers that there are other options besides their usual products. Few put quality above all else.

In this market situation, it becomes almost impossible for connoisseurs to put together an attractive, albeit perhaps limited, selection of cheeses. In contrast, should a restaurateur wish to offer a serious range of cheeses, he or she can turn to parallel sources of supply. There are still cheese wholesalers who are capable of putting together a good assortment. Otherwise, catering professionals in cheese-producing areas can build up the necessary contacts locally. Ordinary consumers cannot. Italy is a cheese-producing country *par excellence* but only an average consumer of cheeses. Italians eat about sixteen kilos each of cheese every year in contrast to the twenty four kilos consumed by the "world champions", the Greeks, and the twenty three kilos of the French. Above all, we Italians are a little bit chauvinistic. For the most part, we eat Italian cheeses, especially local ones. As a result, the range of available foreign cheeses, most of which are French, comes almost exclusively from industrial producers. What to do, then?

Well, we have to be patient, study what guides there are, listen to experts and resign ourselves to the inevitability of having to make do with a **limited range** for our board. Very fresh cheeses should in any case be avoided. You will certainly not find them on the very best tables. However, if you can obtain morning-fresh supplies from a producer, you might want to include a special baked or flavoured ricotta, made from buffalo's or ewe's milk. It has to be out of the ordinary. Mozzarella is not a good choice for it releases moisture and is difficult to slice. If you want to present a particularly good mozzarella – and it must be buffalo's milk –, then serve it with fresh tomato and make it the centrepiece of your table. Next, bear in mind that five is the perfect number and these should include ewe's or goat's milk cheeses, depending on the region. Any self-respecting cheeseboard should have at least one or two examples of *pecorino* (ewe's milk) and *caprino* (goat's milk) cheese. Avoid products flavoured with herbs, chilli pepper, walnuts, spices and so on.

Great cheeses should be served **on their own**, or accompanied by bitter honey (mature cheeses), *cognà* (grape-must preserve, ideal for tangy cheeses) or perhaps by small chunks of pear. When arranging the

The two knives illustrated are used to cut hard Grana cheese. The toothed knife is for scoring the outer rind while the teardrop-shaped one is for cutting the cheese into portions.

cheeses on your board, start with the freshest, provide each with its own knife, and let your guests help themselves. Always finish with a blue cheese (Gorgonzola, Roquefort or Stilton). However, there is no set order for serving milder cheeses. Provided they are more or less equally ripe, you can present them as you prefer. If you do not know how long the cheeses were matured, try them and start with the least tangy.

Should you be able to get supplies from France – where there are thirty seven DOP zones compared with Italy's thirty – remember that you will find the best quality where you see the words *fermier* ("farm-produced") or *au lait cru* ("made from unpasteurised milk") on the label. If you are offered cheese by the portion, investigate further. French *affineurs,* or cheese maturers, are usually highly skilled. Bear in mind, too, that in Germany, Holland, Denmark, Belgium and Austria, ninety nine cheeses out of a hundred are made industrially. However, the United Kingdom still has many good small-scale producers. If you go to Greece, you will find *feta* everywhere. There are twenty Greek DOP varieties but they are hard to track down because production is limited and scattered across the country's thousands of islands. Spain has a good range of cheeses, especially ewe's milk varieties, and Portugal offers some pleasant surprises but these products are rarely imported into Italy.

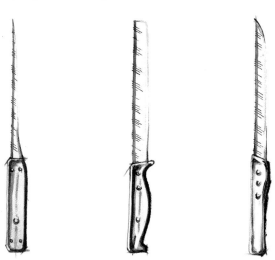

These three knives are used mainly for cutting fresh or soft cheese. The blade surface that comes into contact with the body is kept to a minimum.

2. Tasting cheese

How do you taste a cheese? Can you adopt the same tasting approach you would use for a wine? Should tastings be blind, comparing similar products with assessments for appearance, nose and palate? In principle, yes, but there are some differences and difficulties.

First, it must be stressed that the term "tasting" should in theory only be applied to such operations as have professional, or near-professional, ends. Tasting means acquiring sufficient knowledge of a food product to be able to describe it with reasonable accuracy to another person. The more information we acquire, the more precisely we will be able to describe the product. The question, "What was that cheese like?", can be answered, "Nice", and that in itself is an assessment of quality. But our interlocutor will have gained no information apart from a generic expression of approval. If you begin to describe the colour of the outer rind, the colour and consistency of the interior, the intensity and type of the primary and secondary aromas, the smoothness and appeal on the palate, the length of finish and so on, even without reference to the type of cheese or milk used, you will have supplied enough information for your interlocutor to recognise the cheese on tasting it, or at least compare it with others. Obviously, it is unnecessary to go to the same lengths at home or in the restaurant. But it is also true that if you eat with the same concentration as you would dedicate to a tasting, you will acquire more information – and greater pleasure – from your food. Above all, you will be reinforcing your defences against bad, adulterated or just plain boring food products.

Tasting categories

The theory and practice of cheese tasting are recent developments. They were first formulated in post-war France, and arrived in Italy in 1989, when ONAF, the Italian cheesetasters' organisation, was created. For many years, the DOP Consortia have been applying tasting categories to their products to assess their fitness for sale but the criteria adopted are relatively unsophisticated. Their purpose is to establish that the cheese if free of obvious defects and that the DOP standards are complied with. In contrast, any tasting worthy of the name will attempt to identify the specific taste characteristics of one particular sample at one particular moment in time.

Although most tasters are agreed on the **primary categories** – external appearance, sensations on nose and palate and typicality – of analysis, there is much debate over **secondary** ones – consistency, structure, eyes, oiliness of the body, overall harmony, aftertaste and so on – as well as over **vocabulary**. Cheesetasting poses a genuine language problem for there simply aren't enough "words to say it with".

A working party co-ordinated by Marco Guearnaschelli Gotti met at the Occelli di Farigliano cheese dairy a few years ago in order to draw up a preliminary cheesetasting dictionary. Contributions have also come from ONAF, with its tasting note profile, and from Slow Food, through their regular programme of Taste Workshops. Thanks to this experience, we can now sketch out a first, provisional, dictionary of cheesetasting.

Visual Examination

Leaving aside comments on the overall presentation, that is the shape, the side, top and bottom, which are of technical interest only, the **outer rind** is assessed for **appearance** (thin, thick, smooth, clean, orange-peel, crusty, rough, dry, moist, dappled, cracked or mouldy) and **colour** (white, chalk-white, milk-white, cream, ivory, straw-yellow, wax-yellow, golden, ochre, hazel, reddish, grey or black), the **body** for **colour** (milk-white, chalk-white, alabaster, cream, ivory, straw-white, wax-yellow, orange, hazel, ochre, veined, tending to green/grey/blue) and **consistency** or **texture** (smooth, buttery, chewy, chalky, chalky-crumbly, granular, rock-like, rock-like and flaky, spongy, dry, exuding droplets under the rind, with deep/small/large eyes).

Nose

The taster will assess the **intensity** and **quality** of the **olfactory sensations**, taking into account that it is not just the dominant primary aromas that are to be evaluated. After a few seconds, complementary aromatic notes emerge and these are crucial to the originality, or complexity, of some cheeses. At this point, the taster may proceed to a description of the aromas perceived, using wine vocabulary where possible, or appropriate terms identified specifically for cheese. One preliminary remark: should the taster note a dominant smell of **ammonia**, this means the cheese is overripe. Other critical indicators are **rancid** or **acetone** notes. But while these may form part of the tasting profile for some very ripe cheeses, ammonia never can.

Where possible, we have identified families of smells, listing them from the cleanest to the heaviest, or an aroma bordering on being a defect.

The following smell families can be identified:

cream / buttermilk / acetone, butter / fat / rancid, white flowers / herbs / hay, honey / hazelnut / almond, vanilla / spices, bitterish / ginger / bitter, yeast / earthy, wool / barnyardy / billy goat, sourish / sour / sharp, vine leaf / woody / cheese cellar, cooked / smoky / burnt, noble rot / mushroom / white truffle, cabbage (vegetal) / onion / garlic.

Individual tasters may add to or modify the list depending on their olfactory thresholds and tasting skills.

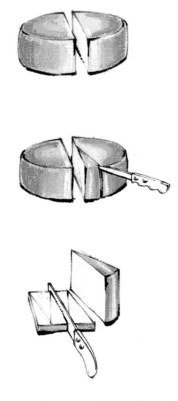

The above illustrations show how a round, high-sided, soft or semi-hard cheese should be sliced into portions.

How to cut a pyramidal cheese. This shape is characteristic of some French goat's milk cheeses.

Palate

Gustatory evaluation should begin with a description of **general sensations** (sweet/savoury/salty, fresh, sharp/burning, hard/round/fat) and the **intensity** and **quality** of the aromas (faint, intense, powerful, elegant, distinct, unusual, milky, bitter). It should then describe the **gustatory** and **aromatic impressions** perceived, identifying, for example, the following notes: buttery / developing lactic acid, sourish, buttermilk, sour or yoghurt, sweet or sweetish enzymes, bitterish/almondy, chestnut, hazelnut, honey, cooked, toasted, hay, garlic, onion, wool, vine leaf, dry, piquant or pungent, mould or mushroom, rancid.

It is then necessary to decide whether the impressions perceived are **balanced** and what overall sensation the cheese elicits. In other words, is the taster's perception thin, fondant or "melt-in-the-mouth", silky, buttery, crystallised or lacking in structure? Finally, there are two other crucial characteristics to be considered in cheesetasting: **length** on the palate and **suasiveness.** Length (short, long or very long) is defined independently of saltiness or piquancy, which can be modified during cheesemaking and are not expressions of the cheese's complexity.

In contrast, suasiveness is very similar in some respects to palatability. Whereas palatability is a quantitative judgement, suasiveness is qualitative. Both, however, are assessed by verifying what proportion of the mouth and tongue's taste receptors the cheese stimulates. The opposite of suasiveness is pungency, which indicates a distinct, strong taste sensation limited to one group of receptors. Suasiveness refers to a much wider and fuller richness of taste and aromas.

A dictionary of tasting

Aftertaste
The sum of the gustatory impressions perceptible in the mouth after swallowing the cheese. The aftertaste is assessed in terms of the quality and duration of perception (see **Length**).

Aroma
The sum of the odorous compounds and scents of a substance, perceptible by the olfactory bulb. Odorous molecules are perceived by a retronasal – not direct nasal – route. Aromas may be animal, milk, vegetal and so on.

Balance
The balance of a cheese is the degree of congruence of the various sensations perceived during tasting. The more harmonious the relationship, the better the cheese is organoleptically balanced.

Colour
Referring to the body of a cheese and, if specified, of the outer rind. Depends on the milk used (neither goat's not buffalo's milk contains the yellow pigment, beta carotene) and maturing. The colour of the body may range from milk-white to brownish. The colour or the rind may depend on treatment it has received.

Consistency
The sum of the sensations that emerge from chewing the cheese, and from its adherence to the taster's palate and tongue, to assess the structure of the cheese (hence the alternative term, "mouthfeel"). A preliminary evaluation of protein breakdown, called "body" by professional tasters, should be made by moulding the cheese between thumb and fingers, if possible. Classified as crumbly, elastic, firm, fondant or "melt-in-the-mouth", dry, rubbery, flabby and so on.

Deformability
The tendency of the cheese, once in the mouth, to progressively lose its shape or yield before breaking up.

Elasticity
The tendency of a sample of cheese to recover its original shape after compression and deformation.

Flavour
The sensation perceived by the taste receptors, produced on introducing a food product into the mouth. Flavours may be sweet, bitter, salty, sour, attractive, unpleasant and so on.

Small, high-sided cheeses should be first sliced and then divided into servings by cutting the slices in half.

Friability
The tendency of the cheese to crumble into small fragments.
Granularity
The perception of small, granular particles during mastication of a sample of cheese.
Hardness
The cheese's resistance to a slight movement of the jaws.
Length
Indicates the duration of olfactory perception via the retronasal passage. In assessing length, perceptions of saltiness and piquancy should be ignored as these qualities may be modified during cheesemaking and are irrelevant to the intrinsic complexity of the cheese.
Liquescence
The sensation produced when a cheese sample melts rapidly in the mouth.
Olfactory complexity
Having ascertained the cheese's purity, or the absence of defects, on the nose, the taster identifies the main odorous components and their intensity. An overall assessment of the nose may be made to indicate the olfactory complexity of the cheese.
Organoleptic analysis
see **Sensory analysis**
Palatability
The sum of the tactile sensations perceived inside the mouth, indicating the number of sensory cells stimulated by the sample and the quality of those sensations. In general, palatability is determined quantitatively from the fat-derived sensations present but quality will also depend on the cheese's overall balance (see **Balance**).

Retronasal perception
The sum of the olfactory impressions perceptible in the mouth after swallowing the cheese.

Sapidity
The quality exhibited by an appetising, full-flavoured, mouth-filling cheese with good length in the mouth.

Sensory analysis
The exploratory examination of a food product by means of the five senses of the human body (sight, smell, taste, hearing and touch).

Shape
The external appearance of the cheese, expressed as a solid geometrical figure of small (in grams) or large (in kilograms) dimensions. Circular, square, conical, quadrilateral, tangerine-shaped, sausage-shaped, pear-shaped and so on.

Smell
A sensory quality perceived by sniffing. Smell indicates the sensations perceived by the olfactory epithelium when stimulated by odorous molecules entering the nasal passage directly.

Suasiveness
see **Palatability**

Two methods of dividing a round, low-sided, soft or semi-hard cheese into portions - the so-called "European cut" and the "North American cut".

Above left is a professional wire cheese-cutter for soft cheeses. On the right, the same operation is being carried out with a knife held in both hands.

3. Conserving cheese

How should you keep a cheese at home? Or rather, what do you have to do to make sure its taste characteristics do not deteriorate? First of all, it is necessary to distinguish between **maturing** (sometimes called **curing**, **ageing** or **ripening**) and **conservation**, which are two distinct processes, although the latter follows the former. With the exception of fresh cheeses, maturing is an indispensable stage in cheesemaking whereas conservation is optional and generally has detrimental consequences for the product's taste profile. It is therefore advisable to keep the period of conservation as brief as possible.

The fundamental parameters that govern maturing are ambient **temperature** and **humidity** - one only has to think of the cheese caves of Valsassina, the mountain huts of Castelmagno, the vast maturing stores for Parmigiano, or even the spotless warehouses used for semi-mature industrial cheeses. It goes without saying that the same temperature and humidity ought to - but obviously cannot – be maintained when storing cheese at home, where the difficulties of proper cheese conservation are compounded by other factors. Maturing involves the entire body of the cheese itself, whether it is large like some Provolones or smaller, like Caciocavallo cheeses. Conservation, in contrast, usually involves sliced or portioned cheeses, so other chemical processes come into play. For example, cheese oxidises fairly rapidly on the surface, which gives the body a brown colour. Processes such as proteolysis and the intensification of the product's taste and smell may reach dangerous levels and UV rays in daylight may break down the cheese's fatty substances and vitamins. Cheese is a complex aggregate of organic substances that begin as milk and acquire a different molecular structures and appearance, depending on the age of the individual type. The life cycle is fairly short and the time taken after initial shaping for the cheese to reach full maturity is brief. And that's it. When the product is overripe, the consumer is no longer a cheesetaster but a vaguely unsettling devourer of smelly fermented milk.

Cellar and refrigerator

The problem of storing cheese at home can be at least partially solved by purchasing from a reputable retailer small portions for consumption within a few days. Only those who live well away from the dry, polluted city atmosphere and have cool cellars, where food products can be stored in the cold and dark should contemplate buying less frequently and in greater quantity. Such lucky cheeselovers might even want to revive the ritual of the gourmets who once used to buy whole immature cheeses directly from Alpine cheesemakers to age it in their own cellars. Every day, these connoisseurs would observe the progress of the maturing process and carefully clean the outer rind.

Sadly, old-fashioned larders no longer exist. The modern equivalent is the section of the refrigerator where the temperature is near – but never below – freezing. There, we can store our slice of cheese, after first wrapping it in polythene, greaseproof paper or tin foil. Slices should be kept separate and wrapped individually. Otherwise, there is a risk of physical contact and the consequent transmission of aromas or mould.

Here is how to cut square or rectangular soft or semi-hard cheeses. The corners will have a greater amount of rind so cutting should ensure equal proportions of body and rind for all portions.

Some connoisseurs prefer to keep hard or mature cheeses separate from softer or younger products. For hard cheeses, experts recommend wrapping pieces of Grana or Pecorino, for example, in an odourless, freshly laundered hemp or cotton cloth, before placing them in a small, ventilated larder. If the body is reasonably dry, the cloth-wrapped cheese may also be put in a perforated polythene bag and then stored in a cool dark place. But check the cheese's state of conservation regularly for blue mould may appear on the surface. Remember, too, that keeping cheese at home is influenced by the time of year. In summer, temperature and humidity may reach critical levels so a refrigerator is an absolute must. Finally, the cheese should be taken out of the refrigerator, unwrapped and allowed to breathe for half an hour or an hour before it is consumed.

Another method of portioning a round, high-sided hard cheese. Note particularly the correct method of removing the rind from mature cheeses. Always begin from the centre, cutting towards the exterior.

A dictionary of cheese

Acidity
The chemical property of milk due to the presence of acids and acid groups. Acidity tends to rise naturally after fermentation, the formation of lactic acid from lactose, and lipolysis, or the liberation of fatty acids. It plays a fundamental role in the coagulation, or curdling, of milk.

Ash
Milk contains numerous metallic components and non-metallic elements that are important in nutritional terms. It is rich in the minerals calcium and phosphorus, both of which are present in a proportion suitable for assimilation by the bones of the breast-feeding infant, but poor in iron. Calcium and phosphorus also help to maintain the balance of caseins and are important factors in coagulation.

Bloomy rind
A bloomy, or mouldy, rind caused by the surface microflora (*Mucor* and *Penicillium*) that generate a grey-white mould. Characteristic of soft-ripened cheeses such as Taleggio and Camembert.

Blue cheese
see **Veining**

Brine
see **Salting**

Butter

The term "butter" is legally defined in Italy as "the product obtained by the mechanical processing of cream taken from cow's milk, from cow's milk whey, or from a mixture of these products". The mechanical operation involved is churning. This entails the agitation of the cream to encourage the rupture of the external membrane of fat and separate the watery component (buttermilk). The removal of fatty elements in liquid form incorporates all the components of the cream and gives butter its special structure.

Buttermilk
see **Butter**

Casein

The most plentiful of the proteins in milk, accounting for about 80% of the total. It is made up of various fractions (alpha, beta and kappa) that coagulate to form curd when attacked by enzymes or acidity (see **Curd**).

Caves

Sheltered, stable, natural environments where some cheeses are matured, especially soft and blue cheeses. Known as *grotte* in Italian. Cool and damp, their temperature and humidity are regulated by cold, moist air entering through cracks in the rock. The caves of Valsassina, for Taleggio, and the so-called *fleurines* for maturing Roquefort, are two examples.

Cheese cellar

A suitable place for maturing cheeses, with optimal light, temperature and humidity conditions for promoting the physiological processes involved in ageing.

Cheese moulds
see **Hoops**

Coagulation

Coagulation, or curdling, is the fundamental transformation in cheesemaking. A number of factors, including acidity, temperature, mineral salts in the milk and inoculation with rennet, cause the precipitation of the casein to form the curd and separate it from the whey. When the precipitation of casein is caused by acidity, this is known as acid coagulation (for cheeses such as Robiola di Roccaverano, Quark, Mascarpone and others). Rennet-based coagulation involves inoculation with rennet and is used for the majority of cheeses.

Colostrum
Milk secreted by the mammary gland in the first days after parturition. It has a different chemical composition from ordinary milk.

Cooked and semi-cooked cheese
A category of cheeses characterised by cooking of the just-cut curd in order to promote separation from they whey, render it more elastic and encourage clotting. Cooking temperatures range from 44-45°C (semi-cooking, as for Fontina, Asiago, Bitto and others) to 54-55°C (cooking, as for Grana Padano, Parmigiano Reggiano, Emmental and so on).

Cream
An important milk product that rises to the top of standing milk, or is separated by skimming in a centrifuge. It is used mainly for making butter but has many other applications in the confectionery industry. Cream contains 25-40 per cent fat but the proportions of its other constituents are almost identical to those of the original milk.

Curd
The clotted portion of coagulated milk, which has transformed from the colloidal solution of casein in sol phase into a gel after inoculation with rennet or the curdling of the milk. Curd is essentially casein in gelatinous phase that has been separated from the whey. This separation is the first stage in cheesemaking.

Curing
The final stage in cheesemaking and the one that determines the final condition of the cheese (see **Maturing**). Curing is carried out in special cheese cellars or caves, or in temperature-controlled cells. It may last for only a few days, in the case of soft cheeses, or continue for several years for some hard cheeses. During this stage, the cheeses must be regularly turned over and cleaned.

Cutting the curd
The mechanical operation of breaking the curd in order to pro-

mote the separation and expulsion of the whey. The curd is cut with a special curd knife called a *spino* or *lira* in Italian. Initially, the soft curd is cut into large pieces. The operation is then repeated until the granules are of the dimensions required. The lumps for fresh, soft cheeses are walnut or hazelnut-sized, sweetcorn-sized for uncooked pressed cheeses and the size of a grain of rice for cooked hard cheeses.

Detachment of the body
A physical modification of the internal structure of the cheese, which tends to become detached from the rind lengthways, forming irregularly shaped cavities. The defect is due to poor handling of the curd.

D.O. (Designation of Origin)
Recognition of a cheese in compliance with Italian law no. 125/1954, the second article of which states, "Designations regarding cheeses produced in geographically defined zones, observing long-standing local customs, and whose product characteristics derive principally from the special conditions of their production environment, are recognised as Designations of Origin".

D.O.P. (Protected Designation of Origin)
Recognition of a cheese or any other food product in compliance with EC Regulation 2081/1992, the second article of which states, "Designation of Origin means the name of a region, a specific place or, in exceptional cases, a country, used to describe an agricultural product or a foodstuff originating in that region, specific place or country, and the quality or characteristics of which are essentially or exclusively due to a particular geographical environment with its inherent human and natural factors, and the production, processing and preparation of which take place in the defined geographical area".

Draining
see **Synaeresis**

Enzyme
A complex organic substance that promotes certain chemical reactions. Milk contains about sixty different enzymes, some of which are extremely important for cheesemaking. The chymosin, pepsin

and lipases contained in rennet (see **Rennet**) are also enzymes.

Eyes

The holes that form in the body of the cheese after acid fermentation, which produces gas, especially carbon dioxide. Eyes are usually small and uniform in size, although there are some exceptions, such as Emmental. In this case, the eyes are large and distributed extensively as a result of the action of propionibacteria, which transform lactic acid into propionic acid and carbon dioxide.

Fat

The principal component of milk, where it is found in the form of suspended globules enclosed in a phospholipid and vitamin-rich membrane. The proportion of fat in milk varies from one dairy species to another. It has significant nutritional value as a source of energy and vitamins. Fat is a fundamental component of cheese, contributing to its aroma and flavour. Cheeses are classified according to the fat content in the dry matter, expressed as a percentage - low-fat (less than 20 per cent), semi-fat (from 20 to 42 per cent) and fat (more than 42 per cent).

Flaking

A defect, observed mainly in cooked hard cheeses and stretched-curd cheeses, in which the body detaches in layers on the inside of the cheese. Flaking may be caused by hurried coagulation, the use of over-acidic milk, excessive salting or pressing or by variations in temperature during maturing.

Fossa

A special three metre-deep, flask-shaped well, two metres across at the base and one metre across at the mouth, excavated out of the tufaceous rock at Sogliano al Rubicone (Forlì) and Talamello (Pesaro). To make *formaggio di fossa*, the cheeses are placed in the wells in mid-August. The wells are then sealed air-tight, to be re-opened on 25 November, the feast of Saint Catherine, when they are taken out and put on sale.

Hard cheese

Cheeses whose water content is below 40 per cent. Uncooked pressed cheeses and stretched-curd cheeses as well as cooked and semi-cooked cheeses fall into this category.

Heat treatment
The application of heat to raw milk for at least fifteen seconds at a temperature of between 57 and 68°C. After heat treatment, the milk should react positively to a phosphatase (enzyme) test. The aim of heat treatment is to reduce the native flora of the milk without altering excessively its cheesemaking properties.

Hoops
Special cheese moulds used to hold the curd after cooking. The curd may be left to drain (soft cheeses) or pressed (hard cheeses). Hoops may be made of beechwood, metal or synthetic resin. The hoops give the side of the cheese its shape and can be used to print marks of origin.

I.G.P. (Protected Geographical Indication)
Recognition of a cheese or any other foodstuff in compliance with EC Regulation 1081/1992. IGP status differs from DOP in that a specific quality, reputation or other characteristic attributable to the geographical area, and the production and/or processing and/or preparation of the product in the geographical area, are sufficient for its award.

Inner rind
The superficial layer of the body, just under the rind, with a more intense colour and more marked taste because it is most affected by the chemical process of oxidisation. In soft cheeses, proteolysis occurs on the inner rind because of the surface microflora.

Inoculation of starter culture
The addition to the milk to be transformed into cheese of selected starter cultures of specific bacteria to promote fermentation of lactose and other components. The main culture media used are milk and whey. Starter cultures are therefore milk- or whey-inoculated (natural growth of bacteria), or milk- or whey-fermented (selected bacterial growth).

Lactose
The sugar found in milk, in which it is the most easily assimilated source of energy. In chemical terms, lactose is the union of one molecule of glucose with one of galactose, and is not common in nature. The presence of lactose in some nerve tissues is

important. Lactose has no significance quantitatively in cheese-making as it remains in solution in the whey. Its fermentation into lactic acid through the action of lactic flora is important because this influences the taste profile of the cheese.

Lipolysis
The breakdown of fats promoted by the presence of specific enzymes (lipase). Lipolysis is significant in the maturing process of some cheeses which are characterised by strong hydrolysis, or breakdown by water, of the fat. In Pecorino and Provolone, maturing is promoted by rennet paste-derived lipase, and in Gorgonzola by lipase from mould.

Marbling
see **Veining**

Maturing
The overall result of various chemical and physical processes involving the curd, determining the texture of the body, the external appearance of the cheese, and above all its final aroma and taste. The temperature and humidity of maturing rooms must be regulated with extreme precision.

Milk
By international convention, milk is defined as *"the whole product obtained from the complete, uninterrupted milking of a healthy, well-fed, rested, female dairy animal. The milk should be collected carefully and hygienically, and should not contain colostrum. The unqualified indication, "milk", indicates cow's milk. Cleaning of material and utensils should carried out in such a way that the composition of the milk cannot be modified in any way"*. The average composition of cow's milk is as follows: water 87-88 per cent, fat 3.4-4.4 per cent, proteins 3-3.5 per cent, lactose 4.7-5.2 per cent, mineral salts 0.8-1 per cent. The milk of other ruminants is also suitable for transformation into cheese. Ewe's milk, goat's milk, both highly prized, and buffalo's milk are common alternatives.

Milk enzymes
Important micro-organisms (bacteria) for cheesemaking because they promote acidity and the precipitation of milk protein into a

solid curd. Milk enzymes are mainly responsible for the taste profile of cheeses as they act on lactose and other major components of milk during fermentation. Bacteria, including milk enzymes, are in part removed by cooking while most are eliminated during pasteurisation. It is necessary to inoculate pasteurised milk with a starter culture in order to turn it into cheese (see **Inoculation of starter culture**).

Milking
The operation of drawing milk from dairy animals. Milking may performed manually or mechanically, and should serve the following aims: to produce clean milk, and to encourage the complete expulsion of the milk without damaging the udder. Milk is secreted by animals as a result of a complex hormonal mechanism which regulates the mammary gland.

Moulds
Micro-organisms belonging to the Eumycota division of the Mycota kingdom, of the genera *Aspergillus*, *Mucor*, and *Penicillium*, which live as saprophytes on organic substances and form an efflorescence with their fruiting bodies. The sometimes powdery efflorescence may be white, grey, greenish or even black (see **Bloomy rind** and **Veining**).

Mountain pasture
A mountain region used in summer for pasturing dairy herds, and where the fodder plants contain flavour-enhancing compounds that give the milk special characteristics. The Italian term *alpeggio* implies the presence of a milking dairy. But there are many other names for mountain pastures, which vary from region to region. Two of the more frequently encountered are *malga* and *alpe*.

Nail
A dark inner rind, blackish in colour. This defect occurs when the cheese contains a very high percentage of fat, and when it is stored in a poorly ventilated room or on old shelving.

Outer rind
A superficial layer that forms on the cheese after salting, ripening and maturing. In soft cheeses, the surface microflora makes a crucial contribution to the texture and taste profile of the final prod-

uct. In other types, the outer rind has the main function of protecting the cheese and exchanging gas and water vapour with the surrounding environment. The rind may be washed, oiled or paraffin-waxed to prevent the growth of mould and the red colouring due to the presence of oospores. In certain cases, such as pressed cheeses, the rind is removed and replaced with a protective wrapping of polyvinyl acetate. Rinds may be smooth, rough, rush mat-patterned, lustrous, thin, yellow, ivory, brownish, pock-marked, cracked and so on.

Oxidation
A chemical process that affects cheeses after prolonged exposure to air. Oxidation produces visible modification of the body colour as well as alterations of the cheese's nose and palate as fatty matter grows rancid.

Pasteurisation
The application of heat to raw milk for at least fifteen seconds at a temperature of at least 71.7°C. After pasteurisation, the milk should react negatively to the phosphatase (enzyme) test. The aim of pasteurisation is to destroy all pathogenic germs and ensure the healthfulness of the milk while enhancing its low-temperature storage potential.

Pasteurisation (UHT)
Heat treatment of raw milk for at least one second at a temperature of at least 135°C. After UHT pasteurisation, milk should present no spoilage when stored at 30°C for fifteen days. Milk is ultrapasteurised to enhance its shelf life, and may be refrigerated or kept at room temperature.

Penicillium
A genus of fungi that grows on the surface or inside cheeses. *Penicillium roqueforti* is the main agent responsible for internal veining in Roquefort, Gorgonzola and similar blue cheeses. *Penicillium camemberti* acts on bloomy rind cheeses, such as Camembert or Brie.

Stretched-curd
Cheeses whose cheesemaking process includes the immersion of the curd in hot, acid whey for several hours to remove minerals

from the body and render it elastic. The curd is then kneaded and stretched in warm water at 70-90°C until it acquires the desired shape. Cheeses of this type include Mozzarella, Provolone, Caciocavallo, Ragusano and others.

Pressing
A preparation process involving mainly uncooked hard cheeses. Pressure is applied for a period ranging from one to twenty four hours to expel whey before a robust outer rind forms.

Processed cheeses
Products obtained by melting cheeses with the application of heat. Processed cheeses are pasteurised and may contain added milk, cream, water, and salts. They have a compact, homogeneous and extremely elastic texture.

Proteins
Proteins are fundamental components of milk whose functional properties determine the basic cheesemaking technique. They are nitrogenous compounds and may be classified into two large groups, caseins and whey proteins. Caseins are found in suspension in milk in the form of micelles. They precipitate under the effect of rennet or acidity.

Proteolysis
A fundamental process in the maturing of cheeses, involving the breakdown of complex casein molecules into simpler nitrogenous compounds (amino acids). Proteolysis is encouraged by specific proteolytic enzymes.

Quark
A fresh cheese made industrially using pasteurised milk. It is acid-coagulated and inoculated with a small quantity of rennet and then cold-chain stored. Quark should be consumed within one or two weeks after production.

Raw milk
Milk that has not been heat-treated, used for cheesemaking. Raw milk still has the original microflora it acquired from its environment. The microflora contribute to the taste profile of the final cheese.

Rennet
An extract of animal origin containing proteolytic enzymes (chymosin and pepsin) that coagulate casein. Generally obtained from the abomasum, or fourth stomach, of unweaned ruminants (calves, kids or lambs). Some rennets also contain lipases, enzymes that can catalyse the hydrolysis of fats and contribute to defining the taste characteristics of the cheese. Commercially, rennet is available in a number of forms, and may be used as a liquid or in powder, pellets or paste. Other coagulants may be of vegetable or fungal origin.

Ricotta
According to Italian law, Ricotta is not a cheese because it is not obtained from the coagulation of casein in milk. It comes instead from the coagulation of whey proteins, a by-product of the processing of cow's, ewe's or goat's milk, at high temperature (80-90°C). From a nutritional point of view, Ricotta is a low-fat product, rich in noble proteins.

Ripening
The stage of cheesemaking that comprises storing the cheese in a warm (24-28°C), humid room for a few hours (up to twenty four) in order to complete the fermentation process and synaeresis (for Gorgonzola and Taleggio, etc.).

Rising of the cream
A physiological process that takes place in standing milk as the fatty emulsion rises to the surface because of its relative specific weight. This phenomenon is exploited in the preparation of partially skimmed milk to be used for semi-fat cheeses, such as Grana Padano and Parmigiano Reggiano, or "Parmesan" cheese.

Salting
The final treatment applied to cheese before maturation. Salt is a preserving agent and an antiseptic that inhibits the growth of micro-organisms. It also has an osmotic effect, the cheese releasing whey and absorbing salt. Salting may take the form of "dry-salting", in which the salt is sprinkled onto, or rubbed into, the outer surface, immersion in vats of brine for a period of time that varies depending on the weight of the cheese, or by the addition of salt to the milk or curd.

Side
The upright, slightly convex or concave, lateral section of cylindrical cheeses. The shape of the side is determined by the hoops used. The sides of almost all hard cheeses bear the name and/or the mark of origin.

Skimming
The process of removing part of the fat from the milk. Milk is skimmed naturally by the rising of the cream (see **Rising of the cream**). The process may be mechanised and accelerated with the aid of cream-separating centrifuges.

Smoking
The process of exposing a food product to the action of certain components in the smoke released by the combustion of various vegetable substances. Smoke is deposited on the food product through the absorption of steam, in which superficial and interstitial moisture acts as an absorption vehicle. Many cheeses are conserved with this technique.

Soft cheese
Cheeses whose water content is in excess of 40 per cent. This category includes fresh cheeses for immediate consumption (Mozzarella, Robiola, Quartirolo and so on) and medium mature cheeses (such as Gorgonzola and Taleggio).

Starter culture
see **Inoculation of starter culture**

Swelling
A frequent defect of cooked cheeses, caused by gas-producing micro-organisms. Swelling is "premature" when it is caused by the fermentation of lactose by non-milk bacteria (*Coli*, etc.) and "delayed" when it presents towards the end of maturing as a result of butyric or propionic fermentation.

Synaeresis
The set of phenomena provoking expulsion of the whey from the curd. Synaeresis occurs more readily in rennet-based than in acid-promoted coagulation since the curd is less contractile.

Top and bottom
The two plane surfaces on which cylindrical cheeses rest. The top and bottom surfaces of a cheese may be flat (Grana, Parmigiano), convex (Asiago Pressato) or concave (some *canestrato*, or mat-drained, cheeses). The top or bottom sometimes carries the cheese's mark of origin.

Top of the milk
see **Cream**

Typical Designation
Recognition of a cheese in compliance with Italian law no. 125/1954, the second article of which states, "Typical Designations are those relating to cheeses produced on Italian territory observing genuine, long-standing customs, whose product characteristics derive from special methods in the reproduction technique". Designation of Origin, as distinct from Typical Designation, is related to the influence of environmental factors in the zone of origin on the finished product.

Uncooked cheeses
A category of cheeses whose cheesemaking process does not include cooking the curd after it is cut. Fresh cheeses and soft cheeses are all uncooked. Some hard or semi-hard cheeses, such as Bra, Raschera and Castelmagno from Italy, Cheddar from the United Kingdom and Edam from Holland, are pressed and uncooked.

Veining
The distinguishing feature of blue cheeses whose body is veined with blue or green mould. Also called "marbling", veining is characteristic of some of Europe's greatest cheeses, such as Gorgonzola, Stilton, Roquefort and other blue cheeses from France. The Italian word *erborinatura* derives from the Lombard dialect word *erborin*, meaning "parsley", a reference to the colour and structure of the body of such cheeses. The term used in French is *persillé*.

Washed rind
see **Outer rind**

Whey drainage
see **Synaeresis**

Whey
The liquid by-product of cheesemaking which contains lactose, whey proteins and mineral salts. Whey accounts for about 90 per cent of the milk used initially. It is partially recycled in the cheese factory for the preparation of starter cultures (see **Inoculation of starter culture**) and Ricotta (see **Ricotta**). Whey is also used in the confectionery industry as a powder or concentrate, and as animal feed.

Whey proteins
Proteins that are not precipitated by rennet or acidity and that remain in the whey in solution. The major whey proteins are lactalbumins and lactoglobulins. These proteins may be recovered in the form of Ricotta, or cottage cheese. colostrum is also extremely rich in lactalbumins and lactoglobulins, the first antibodies to be acquired by newborns.

Yield
The proportion of milk transformed into cheese during cheesemaking. Yield is expressed as a percentage in kilograms of cheese obtained per one hundred kilograms of milk used. A yield of ten per cent is reckoned to be average but the figure may range from 15-20 per cent for very fresh products, to 7-8 per cent for hard cheeses.

Yoghurt
Milk fermented by cultures of *Lactobacillus bulgaricus* and *Streptococcus thermophilus*. Whole, partially skimmed or skimmed milk, pasteurised or heat-treated, is inoculated with a specific starter culture, cooled and stored at 4°C until it is consumed. Sold as a "live" or "living" product.

Abruzzo and Molise

A bruzzo and Molise are regions where herds continue to be taken to mountain pastures, the *gioco della ruzzola* (cheese-rolling) is still popular and traditional cheese flourishes. Pecorino is the most common, the finest examples coming from Farindola and Capracotta, where one of Italy's oldest cheeses is produced.

Cow's
Caciocavallo di Agnone

The milk is heated to a temperature of 37°C and inoculated with a paste of lamb's or kid's rennet, according to the degree of piquancy desired. Coagulation occurs within about 50 minutes. The resulting soft curd is broken into rough lumps and the whey is partially extracted. The curd is then further broken down into tiny granules and left to ripen in warm whey (45-50°C) for several hours. After this process, it is extracted from the remaining whey, cut into slices, and placed in water heated to a temperature of 80°C where the stretching process begins. When the now firm curd has become sufficiently elastic to be modelled into a large pear shape, it is immersed in a brine bath for a period that can vary from between 12 and 20 hours. The forms of cheese are then tied together in pairs and put in a cool well-aired room to mature for approximately 20 days. This is the first step in the ageing process that traditionally takes place in caves, at a constant temperature, and lasts anywhere from three months to a year.

Rennet: paste, lamb's or kid's
Outer rind: smooth, thin, hard, light brown in colour
Body: solid, occasional cracks, straw-coloured of variable intensity
Top and bottom: curved, 16-22 cm in diameter
Height/weight: 18-28 cm / 1.5-3 kg
Territory of origin: the whole region, notably Upper Molise

Formaggella del Sannio

This is essentially a new type of cheese that follows the traditional Pecorino production process of the area. The producer came up with idea of using a small dose of rennet to coagulate the ewe's milk so that it retains as far as possible the characteristic aromas of the grazing pastures. The milk is moderately heated to a temperature of no more than 30°C, a small amount of rennet is added and the mixture is left to coagulate for several hours until the curd sours. When it has reached the required level of acidity, the curd is broken into rough lumps. This ensures that the cheese remains relatively moist. It is then put into moulds, lightly pressed, and immersed briefly in brine. Finally, the cheese is placed in damp, cold stone cellars where the remaining whey drains off and the outer rind forms.

Rennet: liquid, lamb's or kid's
Outer rind: slightly wrinkled as a result of the whey naturally draining off, greyish-brown in colour
Body: soft, moist, chalk-white in colour
Top and bottom: flat, 15-20 cm in diameter
Height/weight: 4-6 cm / 500-700 g
Territory of origin: Sannio

Marcetto

The basic ingredient of Marcetto is over-ripe Pecorino cheese. The cheesemaking process consists solely of the steps necessary to salvage the "bad" pecorino. It is produced throughout the region of Abruzzo, but Marcetto from the Upper Teramo area is particularly highly considered. The ageing process lasts for about a year. Inside, the cheese is pale pink and it has an extremely tangy flavour while the aroma is strong and pungent. Marcetto, also known as "pitted cheese", is characterised by the presence of *saltarelli*, or "hoppers". These are maggots, the larvae of the cheese fly, *Piophila casei*, that grow inside the cheese.

Body: creamy, variable in consistency, pinkish-white in colour
Territory of origin: the whole region of Abruzzo

Pecorino Abruzzese

Rennet is added to raw ewe's milk that has been heated to 38°C, and the mixture is left to coagulate for about one hour. The resulting curd is broken up by hand into fairly large lumps and allowed to stand for a few minutes. This firm curd is then pressed by hand, placed in rush baskets and pressed again. After pressing, the curd is cooked by immersion in boiling whey for a few minutes. It is then dried for two days and salted, usually in a brine bath. After 20 days, during which time it is left in a warm, well-aired room, the cheese is mature. To ensure that the rounds are aged to perfection, they are left for a further month and then rubbed with olive oil.

Rennet: liquid, lamb's or kid's
Outer rind: hard, wrinkled, in various shades of brown, sometimes with a slight bloom
Body: solid, open, straw-coloured
Top and bottom: flat, 14-22 cm in diameter
Height/weight: 4-10 cm / 1-3 kg
Territory of origin: the whole region of Abruzzo

Pecorino del Parco

The method used to produce this pecorino is little different from the technique used to produce the classic ewe's milk cheeses of Abruzzo. In the National Park area, three young producers have "gone green" and are producing an organically farmed Pecorino. Raw milk is heated to 38°C, liquid rennet is added and the mixture is left to coagulate for 20 minutes. When it has coagulated, the curd is divided into nuggets and left to stand for a few minutes. It is then semi-heated briefly at a temperature of 42°C, wrapped in cloths, pressed by hand and transferred to rush baskets. At this point, there is a variation on the classic procedure in that the firm curd is not cooked. The reason is so that the product will retain its natural aroma. It is then salted in a brine bath and subsequently matured for a minimum of 60 days.

Rennet: liquid, lamb's
Outer rind: hard, solid, smooth or wrinkled, brown tending to dark brown in colour
Body: solid, slightly open, straw-white in colour
Top and bottom: flat, 14-20 cm in diameter
Height/weight: 4-8 cm / 1-3 kg
Territory of origin: the National Park area of Abruzzo

Pecorino del Sannio

Pecorino del Sannio is made from Comisana ewe's milk using a production process that differs considerably from classic Italian methods. First, the raw milk is filtered and then heated to a temperature of only 30°C. Only a very small amount of rennet is added so the milk may take up to six hours to coagulate. The process is, in fact, rennet-assisted lactic acid coagulation. The soft curd is broken up into pieces the size of a grain of rice, poured into moulds, pressed by hand and turned over several times in its moulds. When it has dried out, it is dry-salted. The cheeses are then placed in a damp, well-aired cave where they are left for 50 to 90 days. During this time, the rind is oiled regularly.

Rennet: paste, lamb's
Outer rind: hard, slightly wrinkled, very dark brown to black
Body: firm, fine, rather crumbly, lustrous ivory white in colour
Top and bottom: flat, 18-25 cm in diameter
Height/weight: 4-6 cm / 1.3-1.7 kg
Territory of origin: the Molise side of the Sannio area

Pecorino di Capracotta

Pecorino di Capracotta has been produced here since the times of the ancient Sannites who originally colonised this region. The milk is first heated to a temperature of 37°C, rennet is added and after approximately 20-30 minutes, when coagulation has taken place, the soft curd is broken finely into tiny granules the size of a grain of rice. These granules are wrapped in a cloth and partially cooked at a temperature of 42-45°C for a few minutes, then put into moulds. The firm curd is then cooked and dry-salted. This cheese has an extremely pungent smell and a very tangy flavour when aged. It is particularly delicious when dipped in egg and fried.

Rennet: paste or liquid, lamb's or kid's
Outer rind: hard, solid, yellow-brown in colour
Body: fatty, hard, semi-cooked, straw-white in colour
Top and bottom: flat, 14-22 cm in diameter
Height/weight: 4-9 cm / 1-2.5 kg
Territory of origin: the municipalities of Capracotta, Agnone, Carovilli, Vastogirardi, San Pietro Avellana and Pescopennataro

Pecorino di Farindola

This is perhaps one of Italy's most unusual cheeses in that it is almost the only one made with pig's rennet, which gives it a very distinctive aroma. The classic Pecorino cheesemaking technique is used. The milk is curdled at 36-38°C in about 20 minutes and the soft curd is then broken into tiny pieces the size of a grain of sweetcorn. It is part-cooked in a solution of boiling water and whey before removal and transfer to rush baskets. Ageing, however, is rather different from the normal procedure for Pecorino. Once the cheese has been shaped, it is placed on wooden racks in hot damp rooms to dry out. It is left there for 20-30 days until it has formed the characteristic waxy skin, which is hard and oily. The rounds are then placed inside a wooden chest that is opened and closed periodically, depending on progess of the ripening process and to regulate humidity. Throughout this phase, the cheeses are regularly oiled with extra-virgin olive oil until they are ready for maturing.

Rennet: liquid, pig's
Outer rind: smooth, waxy, varying in colour from yellow-brown to reddish
Body: solid, slightly open, from light to dark straw-yellow in colour
Top and bottom: flat, 14-22 cm in diameter
Height/weight: 4-8 cm / 1-3 kg
Territory of origin: the mountain villages of Vestina and Cermignano, and the eastern slopes of the Gran Sasso mountain

Ricotta al Fumo di Ginepro

This very strong-flavoured, juniper-aromatised Ricotta is made with whey left over from Pecorino production. The classic Ricotta technique is used. The whey is heated, sometimes after the addition of a small amount of ewe's milk, to a temperature of 80-90°C, taking care not to let it boil. The proteins that rise to the surface are strained off and placed in rush baskets where they is left to drain. When the mass has dried completely, it is dry-salted and left to ripen for about a week. The cheese is then placed in a closed room in which juniper wood is burned. It remains there for about 24 hours, until it has acquired its characteristic smoky aroma, with notes of balsamic juniper. Ricotta al Fumo di Ginepro is produced with whey from organically farmed milk.

Body: solid, brownish white in colour
Weight: 300-400 g
Territory of origin: the National Park area of Abruzzo

Stracciata

Raw cow's milk is heated to a temperature of 37°C then coagulated in about 20-30 minutes by inoculation with calf's rennet. The soft curd is broken into granules the size of a grain of sweetcorn and allowed to cool for one or two hours. When ready, it is cut and stretched into ribbons that are cooled in water, salted in brine, folded and divided into lumps weighing approximately half a kilogram. Fresh Stracciata should be consumed as soon as possible after it is made. It can be served with salami, ham or other cold meats, or with fresh vegetables such as green salads, tomatoes or rocket. When kept for a few days, Stracciata changes consistency and becomes an appetising spreading cheese.

Rennet: liquid or paste, calf's
Body: elastic, soft, ivory white in colour
Top and bottom: smooth, flat
Height/weight: 2 cm / 400-500 g
Territory of origin: the municipality of Agnone and the Upper Molise area

Basilicata

Basilicata has done its utmost to preserve its traditional cheeses. The region's selection is modest, but it does boast products of great character, such as Casieddu, which resembles Cacioricotta wrapped in fern fronds.

Burrino

Burrino cheese has a double structure comprising an outside layer of soft, springy cheese and an inside layer of butter from the whey. The butter is worked by hand in very cold water, refrigerated so that it solidifies, then inserted into an envelope of cheese which is drawn together like a string purse and tied at the neck before being immersed in very hot water. Alternatively, the cheese may be part-cooked by heating the curd in whey or hot water. Burrino is white tending to yellow or ivory in colour on the inside and straw-coloured on the outside. It has a creamy consistency and a pungent aroma. Burrino made from the milk of Podolica cows is particularly highly prized.

Rennet: liquid, calf's
Outer rind: smooth, fine, lustrous, white tending to straw-white in colour
Body: elastic, soft on the outside, creamy on the inside
Top and bottom: smooth, 6-10 cm in diameter
Height/weight: up to 15 cm / 250-500 g
Territory of origin: Basilicata

Casieddu

Although there is no historical evidence to prove it, Casieddu is generally believed to be related to the more traditional Cacioricotta cheese of the region. The milk from two milkings is filtered through fern fronds and then a small pouch containing *nepeta,* or savoury *(Colomintha nepeta savi)*, a very aromatic herb of the Labiatae family, is steeped in it for a short time. The milk is then boiled, allowed to cool to a temperature of approximately 40°C, and goat rennet is added. After the mixture has coagulated, the curd is cut into tiny pieces, gathered up and worked by hand until it can be kneaded into a ball. When sold fresh, Casieddu is wrapped in fern fronds.

Rennet: paste, kid's
Outer rind: hard, yellowish-grey in colour
Body: uncooked, hard or soft depending on how long it has been aged. White tending to straw-white in colour
Top and bottom: smooth, 10-15 cm in diameter
Weight: / 400-500 g
Territory of origin: the mountain and hill slopes of Val d'Agri, especially the Moliterno area

Fior di Latte

The name Fior di Latte is used to distinguish Mozzarella made using cow's milk from the buffalo's milk product. A milk or whey-based starter culture made the previous day is added to raw or pasteurised milk, which is then inoculated with calf's rennet. Once coagulation has taken place, the soft curd is separated, gathered up and left to drain on wooden or stainless steel tables. It is then subjected to the "stretch test" and, if adjudged sufficiently elastic, is cut and kneaded. The cheeses are usually salted in brine and are ready for the table after only a few hours. Fior di Latte is white in colour and has a soft elastic texture. It is eaten fresh and used as an ingredient in a wide range of Italian dishes, including pizza.

Rennet: liquid, calf's
Body: elastic, soft, creamy white in colour
Top and bottom: smooth
Height/weight: variable / 50-500 g
Territory of origin: Basilicata

Pallone di Gravina

In ancient times, this cheese was made in the province of Bari, particularly around Gravina, hence its name. Today, however, it is produced in the province of Matera. The production process is similar to that used to make Caciocavallo. The milk is coagulated and the soft curd is wrapped in a cloth and put on a *tompagno* ("board") to allow the whey to drain off. When the curd has reached the required level of acidity, usually after two or three hours, it is cut into small slices, and stretched in hot water. During this process, it is kneaded into its characteristic ball shape. When the balls of firm curd have been salted in brine, they are left to dry in the rooms where they were made for about 15 days, then placed in a cellar to mature. Pallone di Gravina can be eaten fresh but is particularly appreciated when matured for a minimum of one year.

Rennet: liquid, calf's, or paste, lamb's or kid's
Outer rind: hard, smooth, solid, straw-yellow shading into brown in colour, greyish-brown when mature
Body: plastic, uncooked and smooth. Straw-yellow tending to gold when mature. May have a few eyes
Top and bottom: smooth
Weight: 1.5-2.5 kg
Territory of origin: the entire province of Matera

Pecorino di Filiano

Pecorino di Filiano has an ancient heritage for it is mentioned in documents from the days of the Kingdom of Naples. The milk is heated to a temperature of 35-40°C and coagulated with kid's and/or calf's rennet in a paste made on the premises. After 20-40 minutes, the soft curd is cut up finely with a wooden tool called a *scuopolo* ("curd knife"), worked by hand and put in rush baskets weighing between two and six kilos. The curd is then cooked in hot whey, salted in brine, and placed in a cellar to age. The rind is golden yellow while the body of the cheese is firm and white or straw-yellow. Pecorino di Filano is an excellent companion for local red wines, such as Aglianico del Vulture, Rosso Canosa and Rosso di Barletta.

Rennet: paste, lamb's or kid's
Outer rind: hard, lined and irregular. Yellow shading into to golden brown in colour
Body: firm, with small eyes. Straw-white in colour
Top and bottom: flat, 10-30 cm in diameter
Height/weight: 8-20 cm / 2-6 kg
Territory of origin: the municipalities of Pescopagano, Castelgrande, Rapone, Atella, Ruoti, Ripacandida and the areas of Vulture and the Monticchio lakes

Pecorino di Moliterno

The soft curd, obtained by rennet coagulation of raw milk, is placed in the traditional rush baskets and pressed by hand to make it firm. The rounds are then cooked in hot whey for a few minutes and dry-salted for a period of 15-30 days. The cheeses are left to mature on wooden boards in a cool, dry room, where they are regularly turned over and brushed with oil and vinegar. The rind is hard, reddish-yellow and lined by the rush baskets. The body of the cheese is soft and white or pale straw-white in colour, with a slightly tangy flavour. Pecorino di Moliterno made in the winter has a higher fat content and a creamier texture, and so is more highly prized.

Rennet: paste, kid's or lamb's
Rind: hard, lined, yellow in colour with streaks of red and brown
Body: uncooked, firm, soft and fat-rich. Ivory-white or brown in colour
Top and bottom: flat, 20 cm in diameter
Height/weight: 10 cm / 2-3 kg
Territory of origin: the municipalities belonging to Mountain Community of Val d'Agri

Ricotta

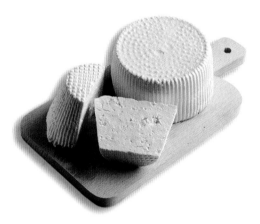

The term *ricotta*, from the Latin *recoctus*, indicates that whey that has been re-cooked. Leftover whey from daily cheese-making is heated to a temperature of approximately 85°C, at which point the proteins separate from the whey and form little lumps that rise to the surface. This Ricotta is skimmed off using a strainer and transferred to rush baskets to drain, usually for three or four hours. At the end of this process, the Ricotta is ready for the table. To improve the yield of cheese obtained, a small amount of whole milk may be added to the whey when it reaches a temperature of approximately 60°C. Ricotta can also be dry-salted, matured for 15-30 days and used for grating, serving at table, or as an ingredient in first courses and desserts.

Body: moist and grainy
Top and bottom: irregular
Height/weight: 8-12 cm / approximately 500 g
Territory of origin: the entire region of Basilicata

Calabria

Calabria is a treasure trove of local and traditional products but suffers from a lack of exposure. Some of its foremost offerings are cheeses, which are interesting though not particularly varied. They include genuine rarities such as Giuncata, Rasco, and Pecorino del Monte Poro.

Caciocavallo Silano DOP

Caciocavallo Silano is documented as far back as the Middle Ages. Today it is produced throughout the southern part of Italy and the following locations are all officially listed as territories of origin. In Calabria, the upper part of the Crotone district, Marchesato, Piccola Sila, Presilana, Monti Tiriolo, Serre, Alto Maesima in the province of Catanzaro, and Ferro, Sparviero, Pollino, Sila Greca Cosentina, Busento and Unione delle Valli in the province of Cosenza are included. In Campania, some of the municipalities in the provinces of Avellino, Benevento, Caserta and Naples appear on the list. The provinces of Isernia and Campobasso in Molise are also included, as are Foggia (including the Gargano and Sub Appennino Dauno subzones), Bari (north-east and south-east Murgia), Taranto (south-east Murgia) and Brindisi in Puglia, and Matera and Potenza in Basilicata. The milk is heated to a temperature of 35°C and kid's rennet is added. The resulting soft curd is cut, left to drain in the bottom of the cheese vat, then put on a board or in a bucket and allowed to ripen for several days until it reaches the required level of acidity. The curd is milled and stretched in hot water, then kneaded and cooled in cold water. The firm curd is salted in brine, a process that can last for several hours depending on the size of the individual rounds, which are then left to mature in a cellar at a constant temperature. The outer rind of the resulting cheese is hard and white, tending to ivory in colour while the body is golden yellow, tangy and crumbly in texture if it has been aged for a long time. Caciocavallo Silano DOP is eaten fresh, but is also an important ingredient in *pasta china*, a traditional dish in the Cosenza area.

Rennet: paste, usually kid's
Outer rind: smooth, shiny, straw-white in colour, shading into yellowy-brown when mature
Body: uncooked, plastic and stretchy. Pale or dark straw-white in colour
Top and bottom: smooth. The larger of the two surfaces is 8-10 cm in diameter
Height/weight: 25-30 cm / 1.5-2.5 kg
Territory of origin: some of the provinces of Calabria, Campania, Molise, Puglia, and Basilicata
DOP status awarded on 1 July 1996, regulation no. 1263

The designation Caciocavallo Silano covers the whole region of Calabria. It therefore includes industrial cheeses as well as products made by small-scale, premium quality cheesemakers. When made with raw milk and very mature, the cheese is stretchy, crumbly and fondant in texture on cutting, with a richly aromatic nose.

Canestrato Crotonese

The first documented reference to Pecorino Crotonese dates from the second half of the eighteenth century. The milk from two milkings is coagulated with rennet in paste at a temperature of about 37°C for 30 minutes. The curd is then broken into small pieces and part-cooked, then placed in the traditional cheese moulds made from woven rushes. The cheese is aged in refrigerated rooms at a temperature kept below 18°C, and at low relative humidity. The outer rind is hard and dark yellow in colour while the body of the cheese is white with very few eyes. It has a savoury, tangy taste. At Easter, Pecorino - or Canestrato - Crotonese is traditionally eaten fresh with raw broad beans and local red wines, such as Cirò, Val di Neto and Melissa.

Rennet: paste, kid's or lamb's
Outer rind: hard, lined by the rush moulds, varying in colour from brownish yellow to a deep grey
Body: part-cooked and hard, ranging from pale to dark straw-yellow in colour
Top and bottom: flat, 20-30 cm in diameter
Height/weight: 7-10 cm / 2-3 kg
Territory of origin: the province of Crotone and the Sila area between Rossano and Catanzaro Lido

Caprino d'Aspromonte

Kid's rennet is inoculated into milk heated to a temperature of 36-37°C. Once coagulation has taken place, the soft curd is broken with a *ruotolo* ("curd knife") into rice-sized granules. When the curd has sunk to the bottom, it is strained off and put in rush baskets where it is pressed by hand. After a few hours, the firm curd is dry-salted, and the rounds are then left to mature on a *cannizzo* ("rush racks"), or a wooden rack in a cool room. The rind, which is white when the cheese is fresh and brownish yellow when mature, is clearly ridged with the marks of the rush mats. The body of the cheese is white and supple, but tends to harden with maturing. The flavour is mild, with a slightly sourish taste and gamy notes. Caprino d'Aspromonte is sold fresh as a table cheese, or mature as a hard cheese for grating.

Rennet: paste, kid's
Outer rind: solid, lined by the rush containers. Varying in colour from yellow to grey-brown
Body: uncooked, firm, white. Ivory-white shading into brown in colour
Top and bottom: flat, 18-20 cm in diameter
Height/weight: 6-7 cm / 1-2 kg
Territory of origin: the municipalities in the Aspromonte area of the province of Reggio Calabria

Giuncata

Kid's rennet is added to raw milk and the mixture is allowed to coagulate for 45-60 minutes. Once a curd has been obtained, it is broken by hand into largish pieces. When the curd has settled on the bottom of the vat, it is strained off and placed in rush baskets. After two or three days, the firm curd is dry-salted by sprinkling salt over its surface. When the salting process is complete, the cheese is placed on wooden boards or a rush rack (*cannizzo*) for about ten days until it is ready to go on sale. If the product is to be matured, it may also be smoked to dry it out. Giuncata tends to go off fairly quickly and is therefore best eaten fresh as a table cheese. Mature Giuncata is also a popular hard cheese for grating over rice or pasta, or as an ingredient in various other recipes.

Rennet: paste, kid's
Outer rind: lined, fairly hard, brick-red in colour when smoked
Body: uncooked, moist, ivory or straw-white in colour
Top and bottom: flat, 8-15 cm in diameter
Height/weight: 3-6 cm / 200-400 g
Territory of origin: the entire region

Pecorino del Monte Poro

The grass of the pastures in the Monte Poro area are rich in flavour-enhancing elements and milk from the sheep grazed there has always enjoyed an excellent reputation. Raw milk is heated to a temperature of 37°C, a paste of kid's rennet is added and the mixture is left to coagulate for 30 minutes. Next, the soft curd is broken with a *spino* ("curd knife"), removed without cooking, and placed in rush baskets. It is then carefully pressed by hand and dry-salted. When they have been aged for between two and three months, the rounds are oiled with a solution of oil and chilli pepper. Pecorino del Monte Poro can be eaten semi-mature after about six months in the cellar, or it can be used as a grating cheese after maturing for a year.

Rennet: paste, kid's
Outer rind: firm, yellow gold with reddish streaks from treatment with chilli pepper diluted in olive oil
Body: elastic, with irregular eyes. Ivory or straw-white in colour
Top and bottom: flat, 15-30 cm in diameter
Height/weight: 10-18 cm / 1.5-6 kg
Territory of origin: Monte Poro, in the municipalities of Ricadi, Spilinga, Drapia, Zaccanopoli, Rombiolo, and Limbadi in the province of Catanzaro

Rasco

Rasco used to be considered quite a delicacy. The herdsmen of the Sila area of Calabria made it from the top of the curd when their herds were in their summer pastures, at the express request of the local landowners. Inexplicably, this cheese has now disappeared. Luckily, small quantities are produced experimentally by the Institute of Animal Husbandry at Camigliatello sulla Sila. Freshly drawn milk is heated to 38°C and allowed to coagulate for 45-60 minutes. The resulting soft curd is then broken into fairly large pieces, carefully wrapped in cloths, and placed in rush baskets, each containing about one kilogram. At this point, the rounds are turned over repeatedly and immersed in hot whey. Once dry, the cheeses are removed from the baskets, lightly salted and placed on *cannizzi* ("rush racks") in a room with a burning fire to smoke for 10 to 13 days.

Rennet: paste, kid's
Outer rind: lined by the rush baskets where they are left to drain. Brown in colour
Body: firm, smooth, fatty. Straw-white in colour
Top and bottom: flat, 5-8 cm in diameter
Height/weight: 5-8 cm / 300-800 g
Territory of origin: once, Rasco was produced all over the vaccarizzi ("summer pastures") of the Sila. Today, this cheese is practically impossible to find

Ricotta Affumicata

The whey is heated to between 85 and 90°C so that the solids rise to the surface. About 10% ewe's or goat's milk is added to obtain a smoother, fuller-tasting product. The proteins are then strained off and placed in traditional rush *fuscelli* ("baskets"), where the mass is left to drain for at least 24 hours. It is then removed from the baskets, dry-salted, and put in a windowless chamber in which a fire is burning. After a minimum of three days' smoking, the Ricotta is moved to a well-ventilated room, where it is left to mature. It will be ready for the table in about one week.

Rind: wrinkled, hard and brown in colour as a result of smoking
Body: smooth, firm, greyish-white in colour
Top and bottom: smooth, varying in diameter
Weight: 200-500g
Territory of origin: the entire region of Calabria. Ricotta from the Crotone area is particularly highly esteemed.

Campania

Campania produces more than just Mozzarella. Although the buffalo's milk version is undoubtedly the region's most famous cheese, we should not forget other excellent products, such as Caciocavallo Podolico, Carmasciano, Conciato Romano, and Provolone del Monaco.

Caciocavallo del Monaco

The origins of this cheese are very ancient. To make Caciocavallo del Monaco, the milk is heated to a temperature of 38°C and kid's rennet is added. After 30-40 minutes, when the mixture has coagulated, the soft curd is broken into largish pieces, allowed to stand for ten minutes, then milled into smaller granules. Next, it is cooked and cut again. The firm curd is left to drain and ripen, then it is stretched, kneaded into shape, and salted in brine for about two days. Maturing is carried out in cool rooms. The outer rind is hard and yellow while the cheese itself has a very piquant taste and an intensely aromatic nose. Caciocavallo del Monaco apparently takes its name from the cheesemaking monks (*monaco* is Italian for "monk") who produced it in the past or, according to another theory, from the name of a tool.

Rennet: paste, kid's
Outer rind: smooth, hard, varying in colour from pale straw-yellow to brown
Body: plastic and stretchy when the cheese is fresh, hard when it is aged. Varying in colour from pale to deep straw-yellow
Height/weight: variable / 2-10 kg
Territory of origin: the provinces of Naples and Salerno

Caciocavallo Podolico Alburni

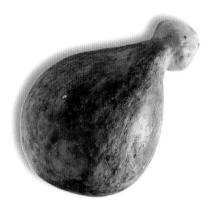

A cheese that has been made for many centuries, Caciocavallo Podolico Alburni is made using a production technique that has been handed down from one generation to the next. The milk is heated to a temperature of 36-37°C and liquid calf's rennet, or a paste of kid's rennet is added. When coagulation has taken place, after 25-40 minutes, the soft curd is cut up into ricesized granules. These are wrapped in a cloth and broken up to extract as much whey as possible. The curd is then poured into whey that has been heated to about 60°C to keep it at a suitable temperature for ripening. This process is repeated two or three times. Several hours later, the firm curd is cut, stretched in hot (80-85°C) water, divided into portions and moulded into shape. The resulting cheeses are cooled in water then salted in a brine bath. Caciocavallo Podolico Alburni is eaten as a table cheese, either fresh or mature.

Rennet: liquid or paste, lamb's or kid's
Outer rind: hard, ochre in colour
Body: plastic, uncooked and tending to straw-yellow in colour
Top and bottom: smooth, 10-20 cm in diameter at the widest
Height/weight: 20-25 cm / 1-3 kg
Territory of origin: the municipalities of Corleto Monforte, Rosciano, Sacco, Acquara, Piaggine, Petina, San Rufo, Ottati, Vallo, Stio and Orria Cilento in the province of Salerno

Caciocavallo Podolico Picentino

Whole milk from Podolica cows is heated to a temperature of about 37°C and inoculated with calf's or kid's rennet. Co-agulation takes about 30 minutes. The soft curd is broken fairly finely and wrapped in cloths, the whey is allowed to drain off, and then warm whey is poured over it to help it to ripen. The curd is broken a second time and more warm whey is added. After several hours, the now firm curd is extracted, cut into small slices and stretched in hot water. It is then shaped and salted in a brine bath. The cheeses have a smooth, thin, ochre yellow outer rind while the body is white or straw-yellow when fresh and deep straw-yellow when aged. Fresh Caciocavallo, and Caciocavallo made with calf's rennet, have a milder flavour while the mature version and cheese made with kid's rennet are tangier. This product is consumed exclusively as a table cheese.

Rennet: liquid or paste, calf's or kid's
Outer rind: thin, ochre yellow in colour
Body: plastic, uncooked, tending to straw-yellow in colour
Top and bottom: smooth, 10-20 cm in diameter at the widest
Height/weight: 20-30 cm / 1-3 kg
Territory of origin: the municipalities of Montella, Bagnoli Irpino, Ariano Irpino, Chiusano San Domenico, Volturara Irpina, Vallata, Aquilonia, Zungoli and Lacedonia in the province of Avellino

Carmasciano

The milk is heated to a temperature of about 38°C and inoculated with kid's or lamb's rennet, coagulating in about 30 minutes. The soft curd is then broken into small pieces, left for a few minutes to settle, gathered up in cloths, put into moulds and pressed by hand. The rounds are cooked in warm whey and dry-salted by sprinkling the whole surface of the pressed curd with salt. After this, they are left to mature on wooden boards in a cool place for a minimum of three months. Carmasciano has a pleasantly full, tangy flavour and a penetratingly intense nose. When the product has been aged for a short time, it may be eaten as a table cheese. Alternatively, it can be grated over pasta, rice or soup when more mature.

Rennet: liquid or paste, lamb's
Outer rind: hard, dark brown in colour
Body: uncooked, hard and firm. Straw-yellow in colour
Top and bottom: flat, 20-25 cm in diameter
Height/weight: 8-12 cm / 1.2-2 kg
Territory of origin: the municipality of Calitri and the surrounding area, in the province of Avellino

Conciato Romano

Conciato Romano is a matured cheese that owes more to the curing process than the cheesemaking technique employed to make it, much in the same way as for Formaggio di Fossa. The cheeses used are obtained by inoculating milk with kid's rennet. The soft curd is broken into very small pieces, strained off, shaped by hand and dry-salted. Once they have dried out, the cheeses undergo a first curing immediately after salting. This is done in water in which *pettole,* a traditional local homemade pasta, has been cooked. The washing process leaves a barcly discernible layer of starch on the surface of the rounds. They are left standing for a while and then treated with a solution of oil, vinegar, piperine and chilli pepper. Originally, the cheeses would at this point have been placed in an unglazed clay amphora, where they would have stayed until mature, a process which could last for up to two years. Some cheesemakers have gone back to this traditional technique.

Rennet: paste, kid's
Outer rind: greasy from the oil solution, uneven, varying in colour from ochre yellow to dark brown
Body: compact and rock hard, ranging in colour from pale to dark yellow
Top and bottom: smooth, ochre yellow
Height/weight: variable
Territory of origin: the municipality of Pontelatone in the province of Caserta

COW'S MILK

Manteca

Manteca is a double-layered cheese whose centre is made of fat obtained from whey ricotta. This is encased in a soft, stretched-curd cheese. Both products are obtained from the Caciocavallo Podolico cheesemaking progress. Whey is placed in a pan and heated until the *manteca*, or "first ricotta," rises to the surface. It is then wrapped in a cloth and allowed to stand overnight. The next day, the curd is transferred to a container known as a *giarra* and kneaded, first in hot water and then in cold, to separate the fat and allow it to solidify. The balls of manteca fat are then wrapped in envelopes of stretched-curd cheese. In the past, this cheese provided a way of conserving milk fat. Manteca is white or straw-yellow in colour, has a mild flavour and is eaten as a table cheese. Similar cheeses are also made in other regions of Italy, including Puglia and Basilicata.

Rennet: paste, lamb's
Body: fatty, plastic on the outside and creamy inside
Top and bottom: smooth, 6-8 cm in diameter
Height/weight: 10-12 cm / 400-500 g
Territory of origin: the provinces of Avellino and Salerno

Mozzarella di Bufala Campana DOP

As early as the thirteenth century, the monks of San Lorenzo in Capua used to give bread and *mozza* to the members of the chapter who took part in their processions but it was not until after the seventeenth century that buffalo's milk Mozzarella began to be produced on a large scale in the so-called *bufalare* or "buffalo pastures". Mozzarella di Bufala is a fresh, stretched-curd cheese made up of very thin layers. It has an elastic texture in the first eight to ten hours after it has been made, becoming softer and more fondant in texture as it matures. Whole buffalo's milk is inoculated with a starter culture of the previous day's whey, obtained by leaving the whey from cheesemaking to sour naturally at room temperature, and calf's rennet. The milk coagulates in 20-30 minutes and the resulting soft curd is broken up into walnut-sized nuggets and left to ripen in warm whey for four to five hours, or until the curd becomes plastic, according to a rule-of-thumb "stretch test". The curd is put in boiling water and stretched by drawing it out continuously with a stick. After this, the cheese is shaped and cut into pieces of various weights, depending on production requirements. Mozzarella is pearl-white in colour, has a slightly sour taste and a mossy or gamy nose. When cut, it exudes a few droplets of a whitish whey-like liquid. Mozzarella appears to have taken its name from the verb *mozzare*, meaning "to cut", a reference to the procedure of cutting the stretched-curd into portions of the desired size. The cheese can be kept at room temperature for between 24 and 48 hours in its own liquid. When fresh, a sliced Mozzarella will reveal a furrow of whey that releases a delicate aroma of buffalo's milk enzymes.

Rennet: liquid, calf's
Body: plastic, soft and springy, with evident signs of leafing. Porcelain-white in colour
Height/weight: 3-13 cm / 60-500 g
Territory of origin: the provinces of Caserta and Salerno, part of the provinces of Latina and Frosinone, and some municipalities in the provinces of Naples, Benevento and Rome
DOP status awarded on 12 June 1996, regulation no. 1107

When Mozzarella di Bufala is sliced, the thin leaves of the inner structure can be seen. A few drops of buttermilk are exuded on cutting.

Mozzarella nella Mortella

Mozzarella nella Mortella is produced in the same areas as Caciocavallo Podolico. The practice of placing these cheeses in branches of *mortella* ("myrtle") appears to have originated with the branches of myrtle that were used to protect the cheeses during transport from the pastures where they were made to the villages nearby. The milk, heated to a temperature of 37°C, is coagulated with rennet, a process that takes about one hour. The soft curd is then ripened in wooden vats for 12-24 hours depending on the outside temperature. After this, curd is broken into lumps, stretched and shaped. The cheese, which is white in colour, has a characteristic aroma it absorbs from the myrtle leaves. Generally eaten as a starter or main course, Mozzarella nella Mortella may be served either on its own or with a side salad.

Rennet: paste or liquid, calf's
Body: plastic, fresh, firm and dry. Ivory-white in colour
Top and bottom: irregular, wrapped in myrtle leaves
Height/weight: 15 cm / 100-150 g
Territory of origin: the municipalities of Vallo della Lucania, Ascea, Novi Velia, Camalonga, Montano Antilia, Stio, Rofrano, Cucaro Vetere, Laurito and Roccagloriosa

Pecorino Bagnolese

The milk is heated to a temperature of about 40°C and coagulated in 20-35 minutes. The soft curd is broken into fairly small pieces and extracted with a strainer. It is then placed in the traditional rush baskets. When it has been dry-salted, the cheese is transferred to a room where it is left to age, sometimes for several years. The outer rind is thick and yellow in colour while the body of the cheese is yellow, shading into straw-yellow, and firm in texture. Pecorino Bagnolese has a piquant flavour that becomes increasingly tangy with maturing. It may be eaten as a table cheese or grated over soup, rice or pasta. Pecorino Bagnolese goes particularly well with full-bodied red wines.

Rennet: liquid, calf's
Outer rind: hard and firm. Yellow, shading into brown or dark brown
Body: fatty, uncooked, hard and straw-coloured
Top and bottom: flat, 20-25 cm in diameter
Height/weight: 10-12 cm / 1.5-2.5 kg
Territory of origin: the municipalities of Bagnoli Irpino, Chiusano San Domenico and Volturara Irpina

Pecorino Laticauda

Pecorino Laticauda is named after the breed of sheep whose milk it is made with. The breed originally came from Africa and was probably introduced to the Campania region by the Bourbons. The milk is heated to 36-38°C and inoculated with rennet in paste. When the mixture has coagulated, the soft curd is broken into small pieces, wrapped in a cloth, placed in rush baskets and pressed by hand. After a few hours, it is cooked in warm whey and dry-salted. The next step is to place the rounds on wooden boards where they are left to mature in a cool, well-ventilated room. The body is ivory-white in colour, and has a mouth-filling, slightly tangy, flavour and an intense, pungent nose. When fresh, it may be served as a table cheese but fully mature, it is also grated over pasta, rice or soup, or as an ingredient in the traditional regional cuisine.

Rennet: paste, lamb's
Outer rind: hard, firm and yellowy-orange in colour
Body: uncooked and soft. Straw-yellow in colour
Top and bottom: flat, 20 cm in diameter
Height/weight: 12 cm / about 2 kg
Territory of origin: nearly all the municipalities in the Upper Sannio area of the province of Benevento

Emilia Romagna

Parmigiano Reggiano – the legendary "Parmesan cheese" – is one of Italy's most emblematic foods. But despite the sheer volume of Parmigiano, Emilia Romagna also boasts other outstanding products, especially soft cheeses like Ravaggiolo, Casatella and Squaquarone.

Casatella Romagnola

Afresh cheese, whose name reveals its traditional role as a homemade foodstuff ("Casatella" is a diminutive of *casa*, meaning "house"), Casatella is made today from pasteurised milk heated to about 37°C and then inoculated with rennet and milk enzymes. The soft curd is broken into walnut-sized pieces and left to stand for a few minutes before it is cut again, this time more finely. The next stage is to transfer the curd into moulds and allow the whey to drain off at a temperature of 20-22°C. The product is then either dry-salted or immersed in a brine bath. Ripening is carried out in a cold store at 4°C.

Rennet: liquid, calf's
Outer rind: the fresh version has no rind. Ivory-white shading into yellow as maturing progresses.
Body: soft, white
Top and bottom: round and even. The top is slightly convex.
Height/weight: 5 cm / 0.2-2 kg
Territory of origin: the whole of Romagna

Formaggio di Fossa

Formaggio di Fossa indicates a maturing technique, not a kind of cheese. Rounds of ewe's or cow's milk cheese are placed to age for about three months in pits at Sogliano, ancient grain stores thought to date from the heyday of the Malatesta family in the fourteenth century. Carved from the tufaceous rock, they are oval in section, two metres wide and two metres high. The cheeses are packed into cloth sacks and "buried" at the end of August, to be "exhumed" towards the end of November. By local tradition, they are taken out on 24 November, the feast of Saint Catherine. The *fosse*, or holes, are closed with wooden covers and sealed with chalk paste to ensure a constant temperature of 21°C, humidity close to 100%, and minimum ventilation. As it ferments under these conditions, the cheese develops bitterish flavours and an aroma of autumn leaves, mushrooms and truffle. It is also very easily digestible. Naturally, not all Formaggio di Fossa has the same characteristics, as these will depend on the type of cheese that was originally "buried".

Rennet: variable, depending on the original cheese
Outer rind: soft, covered with green, yellowish and white moulds
Body: light, flaky and crumbly, ranging in colour from dirty white to straw-yellow or pale hazel
Top and bottom: smooth
Weight: variable
Territory of origin: Sogliano sul Rubicone

Parmigiano Reggiano DOP

Alberto Savinio has written that Parmigiano is to cheese what the double bass is to string instruments. In other words, it is the "keynote" cheese, and certainly the one that is best-known inside Italy and abroad. The milk for Parmigiano Reggiano is collected and brought to the dairies twice a day. Milk from the evening milking is put into broad, shallow troughs so that the cream rises to the surface. The following morning, the cream is removed and the skimmed milk is mixed with whole milk from the morning milking and transferred into truncated cone-shaped vats. The mixture is then inoculated with milk enzymes obtained by allowing the previous day's whey to sour naturally. Next, it is heated to 33-34°C and rennet is added. Coagulation takes 10-12 minutes. The soft curd is then cut up finely into lentil-sized granules before being heated to about 55°C and transferred to moulds, where it will stand and drain for two or three days. The next stage is salting, by immersion in saturated brine, at a temperature of 16-18°C for about 24 days and then maturing begins. This will last for at least 12 months but may go on for much longer. Parmigiano Reggiano is produced all over the provinces of Modena, Reggio Emilia and Parma, in the municipalities on the lefthand bank of the river Reno in the province of Bologna, and in those on the righthand bank of the river Po in the province of Mantua.

Rennet: liquid, calf's
Outer rind: varying in colour from golden yellow to brown, about 6 cm in thickness, and slightly oily
Body: the colour may range from ivory-white to straw-yellow. Flaky and finely grained in texture, with barely visible eyes
Top and bottom: flat, 35-45 cm in diameter
Height/weight: 18-24 cm / minimum 24 kg
Territory of origin: the provinces of Modena, Reggio Emilia and Parma, and part of the provinces of Bologna and Mantua
DOP status awarded on 12 June 1996, regulation no. 1107

Parmigiano cheeses weigh more than thirty kilograms. Note the mark of the Consorzio on the side of the round.

This is the cheese's ID, printed on the outer rind. It shows the code number of the dairy where it was made, the Consorzio mark and the date of production.

Pecorino Dolce dei Colli Bolognesi

The milk is pasteurised at 72-74°C and then cooled to 30-35°C before it is inoculated with rennet and milk enzymes. After coagulation, the curd is broken up and then reheated to 42°C. At this point, the now firm curd is transferred into plastic moulds to drain. The process is encouraged by heating. Next, the rounds are dry-salted and subsequently matured for a minimum of 20 days, up to four months.

Rennet: liquid, calf's
Outer rind: lustrous, elastic and ochre yellow in colour with darker highlights.
Body: semi-hard, firm, with a delicate flavour
Top and bottom: flat, 12-14 cm in diameter
Height/weight: 5 cm / 1-2 kg
Territory of origin: the Colli Bolognesi

COW'S AND/OR EWE'S AND/OR GOAT'S MILK

Ravaggiolo Romagnolo

This is a fresh cheese with a very short shelf life. Once it was made with a mixture of goat's and ewe's milk but today it is usually obtained from whole cow's milk. Rennet is inoculated into milk heated to the temperature required for coagulation and after half an hour, the curd is placed on cabbage, fig or fern leaves. After about two days, the cheese is dry-salted very lightly, and indeed sometimes is not salted at all. It ripens for a further night and is then ready for the table. Ravaggiolo should be eaten within three days of production.

Rennet: liquid, calf's
Body: soft, tender and white
Top and bottom: smooth, creamy white in colour
Height/weight: varying from 1-2 kg
Territory of origin: the Apennine mountains in Tuscany and Romagna, including Tredozio, Modigliana, Portico di Romagna, San Benedetto in Alpe and Sogliano sul Rubicone

Squaquarone

What shape should a Squaquarone be? The Italian name suggests the amorphous consistency of this super-fresh cheese, which is usually spread onto unleavened *piadina* pancakes or flat rolls. The flavour of Squaquarone, which is made all year round, is very delicate and mild. The process involves heating pasteurised milk to 37°C and inoculating it with a milk-based starter culture and liquid rennet. After about 25 minutes, the curd is broken up in two stages with an interval of about 20 minutes. It is left to settle and the whey is drained off. Next, the curd is placed in moulds and the ripening process begins. The cheeses are turned over regularly at this stage. They are then salted in 20% brine for about two hours and a few days later, the Squaquarone is ready for the table.

Rennet: liquid, calf's
Body: soft, fresh and creamy white in colour
Height/weight: varying from 1-3 kg
Territory of origin: the whole of Romagna. Squaquarone from Castel San Pietro is particularly sought-after

Friuli-Venezia Giulia

The mountains of Friuli produce a large number of Toma-type cheeses that differ slightly in cheesemaking technique. The best-known of these is Montasio, the only one with DOP status, while the generic names Latteria and Malga cover a wide range of local products

Carnia o Cuc

In the Carnian dialect, *cuc* means cheese in general. Today, the term "Carnia" is preferred as it indicates the products origin. Carnia is made with a similar technique to that used for Montasio. Whole or partially skimmed raw milk is heated to 33-35°C, inoculated with calf's rennet and left to coagulate for 20-30 minutes. The soft curd is then broken into rice-sized granules, part-cooked at 44-48°C for 15 minutes and the whey is drained off. Finally, the curd is gathered up in a cloth and transferred into hoops. It is pressed and turned over, then salted in a brine bath when dry. Maturing takes place in a cool, well-ventilated room, where the rind is rubbed regularly with an oil-soaked rag.

Rennet: liquid or powder, calf's
Outer rind: hard, firm and elastic. Straw-yellow in colour shading into brown with maturing
Body: elastic, firm and without eyes. Straw-yellow in colour
Top and bottom: flat, 30-40 cm in diameter
Height/weight: 6-10 cm / 5 -9 kg
Territory of origin: the whole of Carnia

Formaggio Salato

Formaggio Salato, or "Salted Cheese", is also known as "As'n", from Mont d'As in Val d'Arzino, where the cheese seems to have originated. In the past, As'n had to be conserved in the mountain-dweller's larder through the long winter months and was made from very low-fat cheese. Nowadays, the salt bath contains milk and cream as well as salt, into which whole-milk, hoop-moulded cheese is immersed. The curd is cooked to 43°C, then cut slowly into large lumps so that it retains a doughy texture. The soft curd is not pressed but instead goes straight into the salt bath, where it will remain for two to six months, depending on the final product desired.

Rennet: liquid, calf's
Outer rind: soft and smooth for the fresh version, becoming harder with maturing
Body: soft, yielding and white in colour
Top and bottom: flat, about 20 cm in diameter
Height/weight: 6-10 cm / 2 -5 kg
Territory of origin: Carnia, Val d'Arzino and Spilimbergo

Latteria

"L atteria" was once the name used for cheese made at the old *lat-terie turnarie*, or community dairies. Variations in fodder, breeding techniques and the natural microflora mean that its flavour varies from producer to producer. In fact, each dairy identifies its own cheese by name. It should be mentioned, for example, that in May 1987, the Fagagna dairy registered the trademark "Fagagna" for its cheese which, like Montasio, is also available in a very mature version. The Latteria cheesemaking technique is very similar to that used for Montasio, although the curd is broken into rather larger pieces that retain a larger proportion of whey.

Rennet: liquid or powder, calf's
Outer rind: straw-yellow in colour
Body: lightly eyed
Top and bottom: flat, 25-30 cm in diameter
Height/weight: 7-8 cm / 5 –7.5 kg
Territory of origin: the entire region

Malga

"Malga" is the name given to products made in the mountain dairies of Friuli, where cheeses have been made since ancient times. The technique used resembles that for Montasio and Latteria. Malga sometimes has a tangy flavour has is due to, or enhanced by, the goat's milk that may used in the cheesemaking process. An Alpine cheese, which may on occasion reveal a bitterish note, Malga owes its charactéristic taste profile to the unique grazing conditions and fodder available in the region's mountain pastures. Normally, the cheese is aged for about 10-20 days, although it may also be matured for a longer period.

Rennet: liquid or powder, calf's
Outer rind: smooth, thin and straw-yellow in colour
Body: free of eyes or lightly eyed
Top and bottom: flat, 20-25 cm in diameter
Height/weight: 6-8 cm / 5 -8 kg
Territory of origin: the mountainous area of the provinces of Udine and Pordenone

Montasio DOP

Montasio originated in Carnia, the mountainous part of Friuli-Venezia Giulia, and takes its name from a group of mountains in the Julian Alps. It was here, on a broad plateau overlooking the southern slopes of the group, that herds were brought for the summer. Cheesemaking for Montasio is defined and regulated by a special consortium, the "Consorzio di Tutela del Formaggio Montasio", recognised by the Italian Ministry of Agriculture and Forests in 1987. Only milk produced on dairy farms in the territory of origin may be used. Once, raw milk was used, which permitted the conservation of the product's natural bacteria and enzymes and enabled the cheese to express its full potential during the maturing process. Today, the increasingly widespread practice of inoculation with milk-based starter cultures and selected enzymes has prompted most producers to carry out a mild heat treatment on the milk when it arrives at the dairy. Coagulation with powdered or liquid bovine rennet takes 20-25 minutes and the soft curd is then broken up into rice-sized granules before being cooked to about 46°C. The curd is then placed in characteristic hoops that impress the mark of origin and date of production on the rind before pressing to drain off the whey. Montasio may be brine-salted in a bath or dry-salted with crystal salt. Sometimes, a mixed system is employed in which the cheese is briefly immersed in brine and the process is subsequently completed by dry-salting.

Rennet: liquid or powder, calf's
Outer rind: barely discernible in the fresh version, becoming elastic and straw-yellow in colour with maturing.
Body: firm, with sparse, uniformly distributed eyes in the table version. Flaky, with very few eyes, for the mature cheese.
Top and bottom: flat or slightly convex, 30-40 cm in diameter
Height/weight: 6-8 cm / 6.5 –7.5 kg
Territory of origin: the entire region of Friuli-Venezia Giulia, and the provinces of Belluno and Treviso and a small part of the provinces of Padua and Venice in the Veneto region
DOP status awarded on 12 June 1996, regulation no. 1107

Illustrated above are several whole and portioned Montasio cheeses matured for various periods of time. The Consorzio mark, with the date of production and dairy code, may be clearly seen on the sides, tops and bottoms of the cheeses.

Scuete Fumade

To make the basic Ricotta, whey separated from the curd during cheesemaking is heated to 95-100°C. When the protein-rich solids rise to the surface, it is worked into finely woven linen bags that are then hung up to drain. Infusions or herbs may be added to the product to obtain a more distinctive Ricotta that can be used in sauces for pasta or rice. After a light pressing, the mild Ricotta is removed from the bags, placed on rush mats and exposed to smoke in the smoking room for two to four days before being left to dry in a special store. It will be ready for the table in about one month. Scuete Fumade for grating should be allowed to mature for a longer period, allowing more intense flavours and aromas to develop. Together with Montasio and Latteria, Smoked Ricotta – a traditional Carnian product – is one of the most popular and characteristic local foodstuffs in the region.

Outer rind: thin, tending to brown in colour
Body: free of eyes, white
Top and bottom: irregular
Height/weight: varying, up to 1 kg
Territory of origin: the entire region of Friuli-Venezia Giulia, in particular, Carnia

Lazio

Believe it or not, most Pecorino Romano is made in Sardinia. And the so-called *gentile* ("delicate") Ricotta made all over Italy is universally known as Ricotta Romana. The origin of these cheeses takes us right back to the dawn of cheesemaking and the Rome of Pliny and Columella.

Caciotta Romana

This cheese is usually made with pasteurised milk, heated to 36°C and inoculated with lamb's rennet. The soft curd is cut first into walnut-sized lumps. The temperature is then raised to 38°C, when it is cut again into smaller pieces. At this point, the curd is left to ripen in the whey for a short while before it is drained for four or five hours in a warm room. Subsequently, the firm curd is pressed and left to stand for 12-18 hours. Salting is carried out either in a brine bath (eight hours per kilogram), or dry using coarse salt. At this stage, the Caciotta is ready for sale as "Primo Sale" ("First Salting"), or it may be left to mature for 15 days and sold as a fresh cheese. Alternatively, it may be matured in cool rooms, at 10°C, where the cheeses are washed approximately once a month.

Rennet: paste, lamb's
Outer rind: only the mature version has a rind, straw-yellow in colour with greenish highlights
Body: white, with very few, large eyes
Top and bottom: flat, 15-25 cm in diameter
Height/weight: 7 cm / 1.5-3 kg
Territory of origin: the Agro Romano countryside

Marzolina or Marzellino

Production of this cheese is now carried out by only a very few farmers. The traditional procedure dictates that milk from the evening milking should be conserved and filtered, then mixed with milk drawn the following morning and then heated to 27°C. The milk is not, however, heated in summer because this is the natural temperature of the mixture. Kid's rennet in paste is then added. After the soft curd is cut, it is left to drain in cheese moulds. Salting, either dry or in brine, is carried out after the cheeses have been pressed. Marzolina matures in two distinct stages. The first lasts from two to seven days, when the rounds are left on wide wooden boards or in perforated containers in cool, well-ventilated room. The cheeses are then washed with oil and vinegar, or water and vinegar, and placed for four or five months in sealed glass demijohns. This maturing process often takes place in oil. The cheese is called "Marzolina" when it has undergone both stages of maturing. The fresh version is known simply as "Formaggio" or "Mosciatella".

Rennet: paste, kid's
Outer rind: skin has a light yellow colour
Body: white, firm and slightly grainy
Top and bottom: flat, 7-8 cm in diameter
Height/weight: 7-8 cm (if cylindrical) / 70-250 g
Territory of origin: the Monti Ausoni and Monti Aurunci hills and the municipalities of Vallecorsa, Castro dei Volsci, Pico and Esperia in the province of Frosinone, and Prossedi, Lenola, Monte San Biagio, Itri and Spigno Saturnia in the province of Latina

Pecorino del Pastore

The milk is filtered and heated to a temperature of between 27 and 35°C, when it is inoculated with lamb's rennet in paste. The curd forms in about 20 minutes and is left to stand for a further 20 minutes. It is then transferred to moulds and perforated through the middle to allow the whey to drain. Next, it is kneaded by hand in the moulds for 20 minutes. Salting is carried out either dry with coarse or white salt, or in a brine bath, for about 12 hours. The cheese must ripen for 20-30 days before it is ready for consumption, after which maturing may take place in the cellar for up to four or five months. During this stage, the cheeses are kept under oil.

Rennet: paste, lamb's
Outer rind: golden-yellow in colour
Body: white, almost or completely free of eyes and edged with oil-derived "tears"
Top and bottom: flat, 12 cm in diameter
Height/weight: 10 cm / 1-5 kg
Territory of origin: the provinces of Rieti, Frosinone and Latina

Ewe's milk whey

Ricotta Romana

True Ricotta Romana is produced only in the Agro Romano area, even though the term has now come to indicate almost any kind of Ricotta, including industrial products. The traditional Ricotta technique is employed. The milk is heated to 85-90°C, until the solids rise to the surface. Farmers still strike the bottom of the cheese vat with a stick, listening to the sound to decide when to remove the mass of protein. The froth is skimmed off and the Ricotta is taken out, to be placed in rush baskets. The addition of acidity regulators is strictly forbidden..

Body: soft, easy-to-spread and slightly grainy. Chalk-white in colour with brown highlights
Top and bottom: irregular
Height/weight: varying, up to 2 kg
Territory of origin: the Agro Romano countryside

Scacione or Caprone

Once, only goat's milk was used to make this cheese and that is why some people even today refer to it as "Caprone" (literally, "billy goat"). A versatile cheese to be eaten soon after purchase, it is generally served in salads but may also be fried or used as a pizza topping. Today, only cow's milk pasteurised at 72°C is used. It is cooled to 36°C and inoculated with calf's rennet in pellets. After 20 minutes, the soft curd is cut roughly for the first time and left to stand for a few minutes in the warm whey. It is then cut again into smaller, walnut-sized lumps. The firm curd is now left in the moulds to drain. Salting is carried out while the product is in this form. After draining for about one and a half hours, the Scacione is ready to go on sale.

Rennet: paste, lamb's
Outer rind: the cheese has a vestigial skin
Body: white, soft
Top and bottom: flat, irregular
Height/weight: 12 cm / 1.5 kg
Territory of origin: the Agro Pontino countryside

Liguria

The region's hinterland has become increasingly depopulated in favour of the coast and tourism-related activities. Yet the health-giving, headily scented pastures of Liguria, once intensively grazed by dairy herds, continue to yield unique cheeses that deserve to be vigorously promoted.

Bruzzu

Long ago the Jacini report identified Bruzzu as a dairy product made from soured and fermented Ricotta. Until 20 or so years ago, it was very popular and produced in large quantities. At that point, output fell dramatically but today there is something of a revival. The cheese is obtained from ewe's milk whey heated to 70-90°C, as is the case with all Ricottas. Unlike other cheeses of this type, the solids are put into moulds to drain after being collected, and thereafter into small wooden vats where they ferment. Salt is added when fermentation takes place but an unsalted version can also be found. The wooden vats are then transferred to the cellar for about a week, during which time the cheeses are turned over every day.

Body: creamy, ivory-white or brownish-white in colour
Height/weight: irregular
Territory of origin: the municipalities of Triora, Molini di Triora and Cosio di Arroscia in the province of Imperia, and Ormea in the province of Cuneo

Formaggetta della Valle Argentina

Every farmer in the production area makes this cheese with the milk to hand, taking care to make a separate curd for each round. Some put the rennet into the milk, then divide the mixture up into moulds while others put the milk into the moulds, and then inoculate them with rennet. The curd is never cut. When it is transferred from the container to the mould, the whey is delicately drained off and the mould is turned upside down while taking care not to break up the curd. Coagulation takes about 20-22 hours. The flavour of the milk, which is traditionally whole and unpasteurised, depends on the pastures where the herds have grazed. Cheeses from the hinterland are rich in aromatic herbs which imbue the milk, and so the cheese, with a special fragrance. Formaggetta is generally eaten fresh but it may be left to mature, sometimes for long periods. Three months after production, it can be used as a grating cheese to enhance the flavour of pesto sauce or vegetable pies.

Rennet: liquid chemical
Outer rind: the fresh version has no rind. Yellow shading into ochre as maturing proceeds
Body: white, firm and soft in the fresh version. Straw-white, elastic and fatty, with small, evenly distributed eyes, in the mature cheese
Top and bottom: flat, about 10 cm in diameter
Height/weight: 2-10 cm / 150-300 g
Territory of origin: the hinterland of Savona and Imperia

Cow's, ewe's or goat's milk

Formaggetta Savonese

Low-acidity milk from one or more milkings in the same day is divided into small cylindrical earthenware containers and inoculated with liquid rennet. It is left to coagulate at room temperature for 8-24 hours. After coagulation, each container is slowly turned upside down to tip the contents into a mould without breaking the curd. The whey is allowed to drain, then the top of the curd is hand salted. A few hours later, the round is turned upside down and the bottom is salted. After another 8-12 hours, the Formaggetta can be removed from the mould and eaten, or left to ripen for 30 days. Today, Formaggetta is produced only in the municipality of Stella, using 90% goat's milk and 10% cow's milk, at the initiative of a local dairy. Predictably enough, it is known as "Formaggetta di Stella".

Rennet: liquid, calf's
Outer rind: the fresh cheese has no rind. The rind of the mature version is thin, soft and straw-white
Body: the colour varies from white to straw-yellow, depending on maturing. Firm, soft with a characteristic faintly sourish aroma
Top and bottom: flat, 12 cm in diameter
Height/weight: 3 cm / 200-500 g
Territory of origin: the province of Savona

Formaggio d'Alpeggio di Triora

An industrial dairy version is made using pasteurised milk but the mountain pasture cheese involves heating raw milk to 37°C and inoculating with liquid rennet. About two hours later, the curd is broken up into hazelnut-sized pieces and allowed to settle on the bottom of the vat, where is stands for about one hour. It is then removed, salted and transferred to moulds. There, it is pressed for three or four days, after which the hard-pressed curd is moved to a damp, cool room to mature. It ages for about three months, but in many cases maturing goes on for up to a year. It is these more mature cheeses that offer a more complex tasting profile.

Rennet: liquid, calf's
Outer rind: rough, sometimes lined by the basket. Straw-yellow in colour, shading into brown with maturing
Body: firm, compact and golden yellow in colour. A few eyes may also be present
Top and bottom: flat, 25-40 cm in diameter
Height/weight: 5 cm / 5-7 kg
Territory of origin: the mountains around the municipality of Triora

Prescinseûa

The derivation of this dialect term is obscure but Prescinseûa is well-known in Genoa. It is a cream cheese obtained by allowing cow's milk to sour, adding milk enzymes if necessary. Once the milk has coagulated, it is filtered through a cloth. In former times, the cream was then placed in small earthenware containers but today plastic or glass jars are used. The flavour is distinctly sourish and reminiscent of yoghurt. Prescinseûa is generally sprinkled with sugar if served at table. However, it is used mainly in the kitchen, where it complements the traditional cuisine of Liguria, for example local baking and Easter cakes.

Body: creamy, easy-to-spread
Weight: variable
Territory of origin: Genoa and its hinterland

San Sté

San Sté is a name invented to indicate a cheese that had long been made in Val d'Aveto but which had become extinct. When the local dairy was set up, the owners decided to revive this traditional cheese. Today, it is made with milk from Bruno-Alpina or Cabanina cows grazed in local pastures. Raw milk is heated to 35°C and inoculated with paste or powdered calf's rennet. It is left to coagulate for 35 minutes. The soft curd is cut into rice-sized granules, collected in a cloth and placed on a table, where it is kneaded. Coarse salt is added and the mixture transferred to moulds, which are then pressed to drain off the whey. Next, the rounds are removed and immersed in brine for two days to harden the outer rind. Finally, the cheeses are moved to damp and cool but unventilated maturing rooms, where they will stay for at least 60 days. During this period, they are regularly turned over and oiled.

Rennet: liquid or paste, calf's
Outer rind: thin, firm and elastic. Golden yellow tending to brown in colour
Body: firm, with a few eyes, and straw-white in colour
Top and bottom: flat, 30-35 cm in diameter
Height/weight: 10 cm / 12 kg
Territory of origin: Val d'Aveto in the province of Genoa

Stagionato de Vaise

The Cooperativa Casearia Val di Vara, set up in 1978, has restarted production of this classic mature Apennine Toma, using only milk from organically farmed herds. The milk is pasteurised, then heated to 38°C and inoculated with a starter culture and powdered calf's rennet. After 32 minutes, the soft curd is broken up in three stages, with an interval of five minutes between each stage. In the first phase, the curd is cut into walnut-sized lumps, then to almond-sized, and finally to hazelnut-sized granules. Subsequently, the whey is drained off by heating the curd to 45°C and then semi-cooking it. After ripening at 38°C for four hours, the cheeses are removed, dry-salted and placed in a room at 10-12% humidity, where they mature. They remain there until maturing is complete, in an average of 60 days.

Rennet: powder, calf's
Outer rind: smooth and hard, varying in colour from light to dark brown
Body: elastic and firm. Straw-yellow in colour
Top and bottom: flat, 18 cm in diameter
Height/weight: 5-7 cm / 1.5 -2 kg
Territory of origin: Val di Vara in the province of La Spezia

Lombardy

L ombardy is one of Italy's outstanding cheese regions,
in terms of quality, quantity and variety. Almost all
types are found, from stretched-curd cheeses to goat's
milk, mature, Alpine Tomas, soft and washed-rind cheeses,
from small-scale niche producers and industrial giants.

Agrì di Valtorta

This is a local cheese made in Valtorta, a small valley way off the beaten track. Whole, fresh-drawn milk is heated to 32-35°C and inoculated with rennet and a little soured whey, hence the name "Agrì" (*agro* means "sour" in Italian). Coagulation takes place in two to three hours and the curd is left to drain for two days on clean cloths. The firm curd is then put in ricotta moulds and left to stand for a day. It is salted by hand and almost always eaten straight away. It smells of milk and has a slightly sour taste.

Rennet: liquid, calf's
Body: dry and soft. White in colour, shading into yellowish after maturing briefly for a week or two.
Top and bottom: flat
Thickness/weight: 6-7 cm / 70-80 g
Territory of origin: Valtorta in Upper Val Brembana in the province of Bergamo

Bagoss

Bagoss is a local dialect word meaning "from the village of Bagolino" in the Caffaro valley, since this is where the cheese originally came from. Partially skimmed raw milk from Bruno Alpina or Pezzata Rossa cows is curdled at 37°C in about half an hour. The soft curd is cut into sweetcorn-sized granules in two successive stages with a fifteen minute break in between, then cooked at 48-49°C. The curd is left to stand for about 40 minutes, during which time it deposits on the bottom of the vat. It is then taken out, put into moulds and pressed for a day. The rounds are dry-salted twice a week for three or four months. Saffron may be used to dye the body. The rind is oiled during ageing with raw linseed oil. Bagoss is also called "Grana Bresciano". It has a markedly aromatic flavour, but is not tangy.

Rennet: powder, calf's
Outer rind: smooth, slightly hard with an orange-yellow colour. Oiled during maturing with raw linseed oil
Body: straw-yellow, with a grainy texture and a few scattered eyes
Top and bottom: flat, 35-40 cm in diameter
Thickness/weight: 12-14 cm / 15-16 kg
Territory of origin: the Caffaro valley, Val Camonica, Val Trompia, Val Sabbia and Val Dorizza in the province of Brescia

Bernardo

A classic summer cheese made in Alpine pastures and generally eaten fresh. Raw milk is coagulated at 35°C, then the curd is cut up coarsely and cooked at about 40°C. The curd is lifted out of the whey and a little saffron powder is added. It is then wrapped in cloths and placed in moulds. The rounds are dry-salted while standing on wooden boards. After about 15 days, they are ready for the table. The fresh version has almost no rind, a reddish-yellow body and a delicate flavour. The less commonly found mature variety has a brownish-yellow rind, fairly evenly distributed, medium-sized eyes and a more intense aromatic flavour.

Rennet: liquid, calf's
Outer rind: almost entirely absent
Body: soft, reddish-yellow in colour with a delicate flavour
Top and bottom: flat
Thickness/weight: 3 cm / 1 kg
Territory of origin: the area around Clusone in the province of Bergamo

Bitto DOP

This cheese takes its name from the torrential river Bitto, a place name which may either be of Celtic origin, meaning "perennial", or come from a Germanic word meaning "bed". The Bitto flows through the valley of the same name into the Adda at Morbegno, where the famous Bitto fair is held. Bitto cheese is made only during the summer months, generally using traditional techniques, in mountain dairies or *calecc*, unroofed stone refuges that are covered with canvas when used. Fresh-drawn cow's milk, with up to ten percent goat's milk added, is slightly heated to a temperature varying from 39 to 49°C. It is then left to curdle for 20 to 40 minutes. The curd is cut into rice-sized pieces and cooked at 45-53°C for 20-60 minutes. The firm curd is then removed from the heat for a quarter of an hour and stirred continuously before being put in the moulds. The rounds are dry-salted with coarse kitchen salt every two or three days for three to four weeks. The outer rind of Bitto is thin and straw-yellow, going brown with time. The body is firm with sparse, "bird's eye"-sized holes. The flavour is mild and fragrant when the cheese is fresh. With maturing, which may go on for up to ten years, the body becomes firmer and harder, turning golden yellow. It also acquires a stronger, more aromatic, flavour, sometimes with a tangy edge. Maturing, which continues for at least 70 seventy days, is always begun in the mountain dairies and completed in the cheese stores on the valley floor.

Rennet: liquid, calf's
Outer rind: thin, with a straw-yellow colour that turns brown over time
Body: compact, with sparse, "bird's eye"-sized holes
Top and bottom: flat, 30-50 cm in diameter
Thickness/weight: 8-10 cm / 8-25 kg
Territory of origin: the entire province of Sondrio, in particular Valtellina, and the municipalities of Averara, Carona, Cusio, Foppolo, Mezzoldo, Piazzatore, Santa Brigida and Valleve in the province of Bergamo
DOP status awarded on 1 July 1996, regulation no. 1263

Bitto can be aged for an extraordinary length of time. Some cheeses are matured for as long as ten years.

Branzi

This is a variant of Formai de Mut that takes its name from the village of Branzi. Raw milk is coagulated at 34-36°C for about half an hour. The soft curd is then cut into small pieces and cooked at 43-46°C for 30 minutes. It is subsequently put into moulds, covered with cloths called *patte*, and pressed for about an hour. The rounds are dry-salted in the mountain dairies, or soaked in brine during the winter, when Branzi is made in the village's co-operative dairy. It has a mild, delicate flavour that becomes fairly strong, or even tangy, with ageing. Despite the shared cheesemaking technique, Branzi may have a slightly different flavour and aroma depending on where it was made, particularly in the case of the mountain dairy version. It is a versatile cheese in the kitchen and an ideal accompaniment for polenta.

Rennet: liquid, calf's
Outer rind: smooth, thin and elastic. Yellowish in colour
Body: soft, straw-yellow in colour, with faint eyes
Top and bottom: flat, 40-45 cm in diameter
Thickness/weight: 8-9 cm / 12-15 kg
Territory of origin: the municipality of Branzi and the neighbouring areas in Val Brembana in the province of Bergamo

Caprino Stagionato

A whey-based starter culture is inoculated into lightly salted whole or partially skimmed raw milk, which is then heated to the minimum temperature necessary to provoke lactic, or acid, coagulation. Coagulation takes about 24 hours. Once the curd has reached a firm enough consistency, it is transferred to perforated moulds without being broken up. The moulds are left to stand for about 24 hours so that the whey can drain off completely. The small rounds are turned over several times and dry-salted. Caprinos may be sold fresh, after ripening for three or four days but in Valsassina it is traditional to leave them to mature for at least 30 days. There are versions flavoured with parsley, garlic, chives and ground pepper. This is the mature version of Caprino, called "Furmagin Pasà", or "over-ripe cheese", in the local dialect.

Outer rind: the skin tends to become covered with a thin mould that goes reddish with age
Body: compact, ivory-white, smooth and moist
Top and bottom: flat, about 3 cm in diameter
Thickness/weight: 10 cm / 300-500 g
Territory of origin: Valsassina and the municipalities of Intelvi and Montevecchia in the province of Como

Crescenza

Today, Crescenza is almost exclusively an industrial product. It apparently takes its name from the Latin word *carsenza*, meaning "flat bread", because if kept in a warm place, the cheese ferments, swells up and bursts open just like bread when it rises. Crescenza belongs to the Stracchino family. It is made from pasteurised milk which is curdled at 37°C for half an hour. The soft curd is broken up in two stages with a 30-minute break in between. It is then stirred and transferred into special perforated moulds before ripening in a warm, damp environment at 22-24°C for five hours. Salting takes place in brine baths. The cheese takes five or six days to mature and should be eaten immediately. It has a mild, delicate flavour and a milky smell. Because Crescenza poses conservation problems, two types are produced. The winter version has a softer, creamier body while Crescenza made in summer has a firmer body.

Rennet: liquid, calf's
Body: uniform, compact, white and buttery, with a melt-in-the-mouth texture
Top and bottom: flat and variable
Thickness/weight: 4-5 cm / 1.8-2 kg
Territory of origin: the entire Po Valley

Formai de Mut DOP

F*ormai de Mut* could be translated as "Mountain Cheese" but it has to be remembered that *mut* in the local dialect indicates the Alpine pastures, not the mountain itself. The herds are in fact fed exclusively on grass, either fresh or in the form of hay, - from the meadows lying between 1,200 and 2,500 metres above sea level. Only during the winter months do the DOP regulations allow the diet be supplemented with mixtures of cereals, or maize or grass-based silage. Most Formai de Mut is, however, made during the summer. The milk is put into large, 300-400 litre vats (it takes 10 litres of milk to make one kilogram of cheese) and curdled at 35-37°C in 30 minutes. After the soft curd has been cut to rice-sized pieces, it is semi-cooked at 45-47°C, taken off the heat and stirred. The firm curd is lifted out using special filtering cloths called *patte*. After being left to stand and drain, it is put in moulds where it is turned over and pressed. Salt is added first to the curd, then the rounds are either dry-salted or immersed in brine baths on alternate days for one or two weeks. The rind is thin, compact and smooth with a straw-yellow colour that shades into grey with maturing. The body is a straw-white to ivory colour. It is firm, elastic and presents widely distributed eyes ranging from very small to "bird's eye"-sized. The flavour is delicate, fragrant and not particularly salty or tangy. After maturing for the minimum period

of 40 to 45 days, Formai de Mut may be used in the preparation
of a wide range of dishes while the mature version, which may
be well over six months old, is an excellent table cheese.

Rennet: liquid, or rarely paste, calf's
Outer rind: thin, firm and smooth. Straw-yellow colour, tending to grey when
mature
Body: straw-white to ivory in colour. Firm and elastic with widely distributed
eyes ranging from very small to "bird's eye"-sized
Top and bottom: flat or semi-flat, 30-40 cm in diameter
Thickness/weight: 8-10 cm / 8-12 kg
Territory of origin: Upper Val Brembana in the province of Bergamo
DOP status awarded on 12 June 1996, regulation no. 1107

*Nowadays, Formai de Mut is produced all year round but the best
cheese is still made in the Alpine pastures during the summer months.*

Grana Padano DOP

The origin of Grana Padano is disputed for both Lodi and Codogno claim to be its home. Today, it is made throughout almost the whole Po Valley, as far as Trento. Grana Padano is made all year round from the milk of cows fed on green and dried fodder, or silage. When silage is used, in wintertime, the cheese is also known as Vernengo. The raw milk from two milkings drawn on the same day is partially skimmed by allowing the cream to rise and transferred to ten-hectolitre copper vats which hold enough milk for two whole cheeses. Coagulation takes place at 31-33°C in ten minutes, and then the soft curd is cut into millet-sized pieces. It is then cooked first at 43-44°C for a few minutes, then again at 54-56°C. When the curd is sufficiently acid and elastic, it is taken out using cloths and split into two blocks which are put into separate moulds. The rounds are turned over several times, then salted in a brine bath for about 28 days. After this they are ripened and aged in temperature and humidity-controlled rooms at 18-20°C and 85% humidity for 12 to 36 months. During this time, the rounds are constantly checked, turned over and cleaned. The rind is hard, smooth, thick and dark yellow or golden brown. It must bear the mark of the Grana Padano Consortium. Only Grana Padano made in the province of Trento can be identified with its place of origin, the Trentingrana mark. The body is straw-yellow, finely granular and breaks away in flakes. There are no eyes. The palate is fragrant, with a strong yet delicate and never tangy flavour. Grana Padano can be used either as a table cheese or for grating.

Rennet: liquid, calf's
Outer rind: hard, smooth and thick. Dark yellow or gold in colour
Body: straw-yellow, finely granular, breaking away in flakes
Top and bottom: flat, 35-45 cm in diameter
Thickness/weight: 18-25 cm / 24-40 kg
Territory of origin: the provinces of Alessandria, Asti, Cuneo, Novara, Turin, Vercelli, Bergamo, Brescia, Como, Cremona, Mantua, Milan, Pavia, Sondrio, Varese, Trento, Padua, Rovigo, Treviso, Venice, Verona, Vicenza, Bologna, Ferrara, Forlì, Piacenza and Ravenna
DOP status awarded on 12 June 1996, regulation no. 1107

The Consortium mark, the number of the dairy and the date of production must be clearly visible on the rind of Grana Padano.

Magnocca or Maioc or Maiocca

This cheese is made in Valchiavenna and the neighbouring valleys, and is in fact related to several Alpine Tomas from various places. Its production technique is similar to that used for Casolet. Whole or lightly skimmed milk is heated and inoculated with liquid calf's rennet. After about 30 minutes, the soft curd is broken up fairly coarsely but, unlike Casolet, is not cooked. The curd is lifted out with cloths, left to drain and then put into moulds. Here, once the whey has drained out completely, it is either dry-salted or immersed in brine. Magnocca is placed in fairly damp cellars to ripen and will be ready after 16 to 30 days, after which it can be left to mature for months, or even a year. The same cheese is made in Valtellina, using the same cheesemaking technique, but there it is called Scimuda.

Rennet: liquid, calf's
Outer rind: hard and compact. Varying in colour from straw-white to grey
Body: compact, straw-yellow in colour, tending to become crumbly with age
Top and bottom: flat, 25-30 cm in diameter
Thickness/weight: 8-10 cm / 10 kg
Territory of origin: Valchiavenna and Valle San Giacomo in the province of Sondrio

Magro di Piatta

This is one of the lowest fat cheeses in Italy. In the Alpine pastures, freshly drawn milk is put into metal basins placed in running water in order to skim it. The milk is left in the basins for about 16 hours, after which the cream that has risen to the surface spontaneously is skimmed off. The milk is then heated to 35°C, inoculated with rennet and left to curdle. After an hour and a half, the temperature is increased and the milk is semi-cooked at 42°C for about 30 minutes, while being stirred continuously. The curd is then removed and placed in wooden moulds, where it is left for two days. Salting is carried out by taking the rounds out of the moulds and immersing them in salted whey. They are then placed in fairly damp cellars to mature. After 60 days, the Magro di Piatta cheese is ready for the table but ageing normally continues for a year or more.

Rennet: liquid or paste, calf's
Outer rind: compact, hard when mature. Brownish-yellow in colour shading into grey
Body: fairly hard and crumbly, with small eye. Straw-yellow in colour, acquiring greenish tints with age
Top and bottom: flat, 25-30 cm in diameter
Thickness/weight: 9-12 cm / 6-7 kg
Territory of origin: Valdisotto and the Bormio area in general

Mascarpone

The name of this cheese apparently derives from *mascarpa*, a by-product extracted from the whey left over from making Stracchino. The word may, however, simply mean "Ricotta". According to a more colourful version, its origin is the Spanish expression *Mas que bueno* ("more than good"), dating back to the days of Spanish occupation. Mascarpone, or Mascherpone, is made from cream obtained by centrifuging or allowed to rise spontaneously. The fat content is variable, ranging from 25 to 40%. The cream is coagulated with organic acids by heating in a double boiler for about ten minutes at 85-90°C and stirring continuously. The curd is left to stand in the whey for 8-15 hours at a low temperature, then removed with cloths. After standing again for a short while, the remaining whey is removed and the Mascarpone is ready for the table. Excellent sprinkled with sugar and cocoa, Mascarpone is also used in the preparation of custards and desserts. It is thought to have come originally from the areas around Lodi and Abbiategrasso.

Rennet: tartaric, citric or acetic acid
Body: creamy, soft and white with a mild creamy flavour, souring slightly after a few days
Thickness/weight: variable
Territory of origin: the entire region of Lombardy

Pannerone Lodigiano

The name Pannerone derives from the word *panera*, which in the Milanese dialect means "cream". Raw milk is heated to 28-32°C and curdled in about 30 minutes. The curd is then broken up in two stages. First, it is cut into largish lumps and then, after being left to stand, into sweetcorn-sized lumps. The curd is stirred continuously and kept hot until it is removed using cloths known as *patte*. The curd is then ripened at 26°C until the whey has drained off completely. The curd is then milled and put into moulds, where it is left for four days. When the rounds are taken out of the moulds, they are wrapped in special paper, bound in wooden hoops, and placed in cold storage to mature for about 15 days at 8-10°C. Pannerone Lodigiano is an unsalted cheese and is sometimes also called white Gorgonzola, since it is the same size as a Gorgonzola, but without the mould.

Rennet: liquid, calf's
Outer rind: moist, thin with a reddish-yellow colour
Body: crumbly, not compact, with small, unevenly distributed cracks. Ivory-white in colour
Top and bottom: flat, 25-30 cm in diameter
Thickness/weight: 20 cm / 10-12 kg
Territory of origin: the municipality of Lodi and adjoining areas

Provolone Valpadana DOP

Provolone originally comes from Southern Italy, where it is a traditional cheese. Production had already spread to the Po Valley, and the area between Brescia and Cremona in particular, by the end of the nineteenth century. Its name derives from the Neapolitan word *prova* or *provola*, used to indicate fresh samples of dairy products for tasting. Whole pasteurised milk is curdled at 37°C in 15 minutes. The curd is then cut into sweetcorn-size lumps and cooked at 49-50°C. When the curd has reached the right consistency, it is kneaded and stretched in hot water at 70°C. It is then shaped and cooled. Provolone Valpadana is sold in various formats, including salami-shaped, melon-shaped, truncated cone, pear-shaped and flask-shaped (like a pear with a ball on top). Weight and size vary for each shape. The cheeses are salted in brine and left to ripen for about 20 days. Maturing is carried out by tying the cheeses with string and hanging them on special supports. The rind is smooth, thin, shiny and golden while the body is firm and may have faint, widely scattered eyes. Slight flaking is considered acceptable. Provolone Valpadana is straw-white in colour with a delicate flavour when up to three months old. This is the mild version, made using calf's rennet. The flavour tends to become tangy with ageing, or if the cheese is the strong version, curdled with kid's or lamb's rennet, or both. It is an excellent table cheese, and is also sold in a smoked variety. Provolone Valpadana is a versatile cooking cheese thanks to its stretchy texture and ability to melt and mingle with other ingredients. It is made in several regions of North Italy. In Lombardy, it is found throughout the provinces of Cremona and Brescia, and in some parts of the provinces of Bergamo, Mantua and Milan. In the Veneto, Provolone is made in the provinces of Verona, Vicenza, Rovigo and Padua, in Emilia Romagna it is found all over the province of Piacenza while in Trentino it is made in many municipalities in the province of Trento.

Rennet: paste, kid's or lamb's for the tangy version, liquid, calf's for the mild
Outer rind: smooth, thin, lustrous and golden
Body: firm in texture. May have faint, sparsely distributed eyes
Top and bottom: variable, depending on the shape
Weight: up to 100 kg
Territory of origin: the provinces of Cremona, Brescia, Verona, Vicenza, Rovigo, Padua and Piacenza, and some parts of the provinces of Bergamo, Mantua, Milan and Trento
DOP status awarded on 12 June 1996, regulation no. 1107

Provolone is the cheese with the greatest variety of shapes and weights, which proves its extremely ancient origins and its deep roots. Each local community where it was made developed its own characteristic shape. Note the typical flaking of the elastic body when mature.

Quartirolo Lombardo DOP

The name "Quartirolo" derives from the feed given to the cattle during the cheesemaking period and refers to fresh fodder from the fourth cut, the *quartirolo*, which is richer in fragrance and flavour. It used to be called "Stracchino Quartirolo della Val Taleggio", or "Quartirolo di Monte". Today, it can be produced all year round, but the best Quartirolo is still made in the autumn, from early September to the end of October. Quartirolo contains whole or part-skimmed cow's milk from two or more milkings. Coagulation takes place at a temperature of around 35-40°C in 25 minutes. The curd is cut into hazelnut-sized lumps in two stages that depend on the changing level of acidity in the whey. The curd and whey is then put into moulds and ripened at 26-28°C for 4-24 hours. Salting can be dry or by soaking in brine. Soft Quartirolo matures in 5-30 days. After 30 days' ageing, it can be labelled "mature". Quartirolo di Monte is the version made in mountain dairies using milk fresh from the cow, and without added enzymes. It is ripened in a naturally warm, damp environment and dry-salted. The rind is thin and pinkish white in the case of young cheeses and a reddish grey-green in the case of more mature cheeses. The body is compact and presents small lumps. It is normal for small pieces to break away. Crumbly and soft, it acquires a melt-in-the-mouth texture as it ages. The colour varies from white to straw-yellow with maturing. On the palate, it is slightly sour when young, becoming more aromatic and faintly bitterish with ageing.

Rennet: liquid, calf's
Outer rind: thin and pinkish white when young, shading into reddish grey-green with maturity.
Body: firm, slightly lumpy, crumbly and soft, acquiring a melt-in-the-mouth texture as it ages.
Top and bottom: flat, with 18-22 cm sides
Thickness/weight: 4-8 cm / 1.5-3.5 kg
Territory of origin: throughout the provinces of Brescia, Bergamo, Como, Cremona, Milan, Pavia and Varese
DOP status awarded on 12 June 1996, regulation no. 1107

Quartirolo may be eaten very fresh, when it is almost completely rindless.

When mature, Quartirolo resembles Taleggio in appearance.

Salva

This cheese used to be made in May with the excess milk that is produced at that time of year. Salva (literally, "it saves" in Italian) was therefore an appropriate name for a cheese which represented an economic lifeline for many dairies. The cheesemaking technique is the same as for Quartirolo but the milk is processed at a higher level of acidity and the curd is cut into very small pieces. Pasteurised partially skimmed milk is curdled at 36°C for about 30 minutes. The curd is broken up in two stages with a break of 10-15 minutes in between. After being left to stand for a short while, it is taken out and placed in moulds. The rounds are then ripened at 25-30°C for 18 to 24 hours. Next, they are then left to age in cool rooms for a month. At this point, the cheeses are ready for eating or further maturing. Salva has a delicate flavour when young, acquiring aromatic notes of "autumn leaves" as it matures.

Rennet: liquid, calf's
Outer rind: fairly thick. Hazel in colour, shading into dark brown with age
Body: tiny, almost imperceptible eyes. May present slight flaking. Straw-white in colour
Top and bottom: flat, with 20-23 cm sides
Thickness/weight: 10-18 cm / 3-4 kg
Territory of origin: the Franciacorta district in the province of Brescia and a few municipalities around Bergamo and Cremona

Scimudin

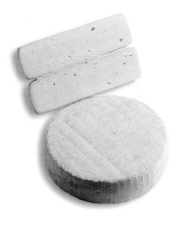

Scimudin is a smaller, and usually creamier, version of Scimuda. Pasteurised cow's milk is inoculated with a milk-based starter culture and heated to induce coagulation. The curd is broken up coarsely and poured into moulds, where it is left until the whey has drained off completely. Once dry, the firm curd is removed from the hoops, dry-salted and immersed in brine. It is then transferred to ripening rooms, where it is left at a temperature of 3-6°C in 85-90% humidity for a minimum of three or four weeks.

Rennet: liquid, calf's
Outer rind: thin, covered with a thin layer of greyish-white mould
Body: firm and soft, with very small eyes. Straw-white in colour
Top and bottom: flat or convex, 18-22 cm in diameter
Thickness/weight: 4-5 cm / 1.3-1.7 kg
Territory of origin: Upper Valtellina

Semigrasso d'Alpe or Livigno

In some mountain diaries, cheesemakers mix cow's milk with goat's milk, which gives the cheese a special, tangy flavour. In most cases, however, only cow's milk is used. It is heated to 37°C and inoculated with calf's or lamb's rennet. After coagulation, the mixture is left to stand so that the curd (or *scimuda*) separates from the whey. The curd is then cut using either a coarse or a fine *lira*, a wire cheese knife, according to the eye size required, and semi-cooked at 47°C, while being stirred continuously. This is the most critical stage of cheesemaking since the curd must be cooked slowly and carefully on a low heat for two hours or more. It is then taken out, placed in moulds and dry-salted or soaked in brine. Ripening may continue for as long as 60 days, while maturing can last for a year or more. Semigrasso d'Alpe may be eaten fresh, after three months' maturing, semi-mature after six months, when it is at its best, according to the experts, or in the hard version after 18 months' ageing.

Rennet: liquid calf's or lamb's
Outer rind: hard and compact. Varying in colour, according to the period of maturing
Body: straw-yellow and medium-hard, with characteristically close-packed, evenly distributed, "bird's eye"-sized holes
Top and bottom: flat, 30-40 cm in diameter
Thickness/weight: 8-12 cm / 8-14 kg
Territory of origin: Bormio, Livigno and all over Upper Valtellina

Silter

In Val Camonica, "Silter" is the name for the storeroom where cheeses are kept and matured. During the summer season, Silter cheese is made using traditional techniques in mountain dairies whereas in winter, it is produced in the small dairies on the valley floor. The milk from the morning and evening milkings, or from several milkings, is curdled raw at around 30-32°C in 40 minutes. The curd is cut and cooked at 46°C for about half an hour. After being left to stand for a short while, the curd is poured into moulds, where it is left for four days. The rounds are dry-salted. Silter ripens in 10 days, but only acquires the consistency of an excellent table cheese after six months. When Silter has been matured for one year, it can be used as a grating cheese.

Rennet: liquid, calf's
Outer rind: thick and brown in colour
Body: firm, straw-yellow in colour, with large sparsely distributed eyes
Top and bottom: flat, 40-45 cm in diameter
Thickness/weight: 10-15 cm / 8-14 kg
Territory of origin: Val Camonica, Saviore dell'Adamello and Ponte di Legno in the province of Brescia

Stracchino Tipico

Once upon a time, Stracchino used to be made in the autumn from the milk of cows that were exhausted (*stracca* means "tired" in the local dialect) after walking for many hours from their summer pastures to the flatlands. According to another version, it was not the animals that were weary but the milk they gave on the water-meadows of the Lombardy plains. Raw milk is curdled at 30°C for about half an hour and the curd cut into slices of varying thicknesses. It is lifted out with cloths, drained and put into moulds, where it stays for a few days. The rounds are ripened on rush matting and are dry-salted. After a few days, the cheese is ready to be eaten. The fresh, creamy Straness version is eaten as soon as it is made while Stracchino dei Campelli is eaten after 15 to 20 days' ageing to bring out its special aroma, enhanced by the rhododendron flowers among which it matures. It has a melt-in-the-mouth texture and a sweet flavour with aromatic notes.

Rennet: liquid, calf's
Outer rind: barely discernible skin
Body: uniform and buttery with a white or pale yellow colour and no eyes
Top and bottom: flat with 20-25 cm long sides or diameter
Thickness/weight: 5 cm / variable
Territory of origin: originally throughout the region but the production area is now much more limited. Stracchino di Nesso from the province of Como and Stracchino della Valle dei Campelli from the province of Bergamo are particularly well-known

Strachitund

Strachitund is a round Stracchino, as distinct from the square version or Taleggio. Its production is still very much a family affair and follows the ancient *a due paste*, or "two-curd", technique that induces marbling. The same technique is also used to make two-curd Gorgonzola. The amalgamation of the hot morning curd with the cold evening curd promotes the formation of mould. On the whole, Strachitund follows the cheesemaking technique used for Taleggio. Nevertheless, it differs from that cheese in that it has a more aromatic, mouth-filling flavour and an attractive nose of "autumn leaves" and hazelnuts. Strachitund is also called "Naturale di Locatelli" and "Erborinato di Artavaggio". The reason for this is simple. Guglielmo Locatelli from Reggetto di Vedeseta in the province of Bergamo is the only cheesemaker today who makes this type of Stracchino and Artavaggio is the Alpine pasture where his cows graze. About one hundred rounds of Strachitund are made each year.

Rennet: liquid, calf's
Outer rind: wrinkled and thin. Light brown in colour
Body: aromatic and mouth-filling. Pale or deep straw-yellow in colour
Top and bottom: flat, 25 cm in diameter
Thickness/weight: 15-18 cm / 4-5 kg
Territory of origin: the Upper Val Taleggio, Artavaggio in the province of Lecco and Reggetto di Vedeseta in the province of Bergamo

Taleggio DOP

This cheese originally seems to have been made in Val Taleggio, in the Upper Bergamo area, during the tenth and eleventh centuries. However, the name Taleggio has only been used since the early twentieth century. Taleggio cheeses matured in the caves of Valsassina, in the province of Como, are particularly renowned. Thanks to deep fractures in the rocks, these caves have a unique mesoclimate that favours maturation and the growth of moulds on the rind. It is estimated that about a third of all Taleggio is matured in the mountains. Raw or pasteurised milk is curdled at 30-36°C for 20-25 minutes. The curd is broken up into hazelnut-sized lumps in two stages with a 5 to 10 minute break in between. It is then poured into moulds and ripened at 22-25°C. The squares are either dry-salted or soaked in brine. Maturation lasts for 25 to 40 days at a controlled temperature of 3-8°C and humidity of 85-90%. During this period, the cheeses are sponged down with brine to prevent unwanted moulds from growing and to give the rind its classic pink colour. The rind itself is thin, yellowish or pink in colour, and covered in bloom from the special moulds that grow during ageing. The body is soft, with only a few eyes. Its straw-white colour is deeper under the rind because of the breakdown of proteins that takes place in the mature cheese. Mild and buttery on the palate, Taleggio develops a fuller, tangier flavour with prolonged maturing.

Rennet: liquid, calf's
Outer rind: thin and covered in bloom from the moulds which grow during ageing. Yellow or pinkish in colour
Body: soft, with only a few eyes. Straw-white in colour, deeper under the rind because of the breakdown of proteins that takes place in the mature cheese
Top and bottom: flat, with 18-25 cm sides
Thickness/weight: 5-7 cm / 1.7-2.2 kg
Territory of origin: the whole of the provinces of Bergamo, Brescia, Como, Cremona, Milan and Pavia in Lombardy, Treviso in the Veneto, and Novara in Piedmont
DOP status awarded on 12 June 1996, regulation no. 1107

Taleggio is one of the very few washed-rind Italian cheeses. In order to mature properly, it must be conserved in cool, damp caves.

Torta

Torta is made almost everywhere in Lombardy. Whole milk, with a little fresh cream added, is curdled very slowly in about 24 hours. Very little rennet is used. The curd is cooked at 45°C and then placed on cloths arranged in layers inside special boxes with holes to allow the whey to drain out. Before being put into moulds, salt is added directly to the curd. Torta is sold very fresh, wrapped in tinfoil or parchment. It has a mild, delicate flavour.

Rennet: liquid, calf's
Outer rind: barely discernible skin
Body: white, soft and not very firm
Top and bottom: flat, smooth and variable
Thickness/weight: variable / 3 kg
Territory of origin: the entire region

Valtellina Casera DOP

Valtellina has a wealth of unique local products that have survived to the present day thanks to the valley's isolated position. Valtellina cheeses reflect the special nature of cattle-farming in the area, which has a macroclimate that is unlike any other anywhere else in the Alps. At the end of the eighteenth century, a version of Bitto, the large-format cheese which keeps well and has better flavour and more character than many others, became the standard product on the valley floor. It was this cheese that today is known as Valtellina Casera.

It is made from Bruna Alpina cow's milk from two milkings, although it may come from more than two milkings if the milk is refrigerated. The milk is left to stand for 12 hours, to permit the spontaneous growth of microflora, and then partially skimmed by allowing the cream to rise. It is heated to 37°C and inoculated with calf's rennet. The curd is cut into sweetcorn-sized lumps and then half-cooked at a temperature of 44°C for about 30 minutes. The firm curd is next left to stand in the whey for a while before being taken out and put into moulds. Traditionally, moulds were made of wood but in modern dairies they have been replaced with food-safe plastic. The rounds are then slowly pressed for 8-12 hours before being taken out and either dry-salted or soaked in brine. At this point, Valtellina Casera is ready for maturing, which takes place in rooms with a minimum of 80% humidity, at a temperature of between 6 and 16°C. Maturing takes a minimum of 60 days.

Rennet: liquid, calf's
Outer rind: firm. Straw-yellow in colour, shading into grey-brown
Body: firm and elastic. Straw-white colour with sparsely distributed eyes
Top and bottom: flat, 30-45 cm in diameter
Thickness/weight: 8-10 cm / 7-12 kg
Territory of origin: the entire province of Sondrio
DOP status awarded on 1 July 1996, regulation no. 1263

Casera is the valley-bottom cheese made in Valtellina. Its an excellent table cheese and may be eaten either fresh or medium-mature.

Zincarlin or Cingherlino

This cheese used to be made from rennet-coagulated goat's milk and was eaten fresh with oil and pepper. Today it is made with cow's milk. Raw milk is heated to 30-32°C and inoculated with liquid calf's rennet. After coagulation, the curd is broken up roughly into four with a cross cut and left to stand for 10 to 20 minutes. The curd is then gently lifted out and placed in containers that may have a wide range of shapes. For at least 24 hours, the moulds are topped up continually as the whey drains off. The cheeses are then placed on a wooden table or straw matting and left to drain completely. And at this point, they are then ready for the table.

Rennet: liquid, calf's
Body: soft, not very compact, fatty and fresh. Brownish-white in colour
Top and bottom: variable
Thickness/weight: variable
Territory of origin: the Besozzo area and the area around Monte Generoso in the province of Varese

Marche

The region has made a serious commitment to the laudable enterprise of rescuing and promoting its cheesemaking heritage. This includes a number of unique specialities that are seriously endangered, if not actually extinct, such as Slattato, Cacio Limone, Ambra di Talamello and Casècc.

Ambra di Talamello

Ambra di Talamello is a "Formaggio di Fossa", made with Pecorino and soft Caciotta cheeses from Montefeltro left to mature in the pits at Talamello. The name was invented by Tonino Guerra and refers to the colour the product acquires during the maturing process. Pecorino, Caprino and Caciotta cheeses a couple of months old are packed into natural fibre (cotton or hemp) sacks between the middle of July and the end of August, then buried in large straw-lined pits dug into the tufaceous rock. The openings are closed with wooden covers and then sealed with chalk paste. They will re-opened at the end of November. The product that emerges is distinctly tangy, especially if made from goat's milk, and has an intensely aromatic nose.

Rennet: variable, depending on the original cheese
Outer rind: soft, covered with green, yellowish and white mould
Body: light, flaky and crumbly, ranging in colour from dirty white to straw-yellow or pale hazel
Top and bottom: irregular
Weight: 0.8-2 kg
Territory of origin: the municipality of Talamello

Cacio a Forma di Limone

Cacio a Forma di Limone, the characteristic cheese of the Metauro valley, is born from the union of two apparently in-compatible components – milk and lemon. It is made only with ewe's milk from the local area, inoculated with natural rennet, again local, and involves a relatively fast cheesemaking process. The soft curd is broken up delicately, either by hand or with spe-cial tools, into medium-sized granules and then left to stand in the whey for a few minutes before being transferred into lemon-shaped moulds. It is dry-salted with a mixture of salt and grated zest of lemon. The excess salt is removed and the cheese is washed. The next stage is to brush the cheeses with flour and water to en-able the lemon rind to adhere to the surface. The product is then matured in a cool, damp room for a period of four to ten days.

Rennet: paste, lamb's
Outer rind: the outer surface of the cheeses is covered in lemon rind
Body: fresh, white, with a lemony flavour
Top and bottom: smooth, curved
Height/weight: variable / 100-150 g
Territory of origin: the valley of the Metauro

Goat's and cow's milk
Casciotta di Urbino DOP

The origins of Casciotta di Urbino are extremely ancient. It has had many famous admirers, including Pope Clement XIV and Michelangelo. There is a sort of folk legend that attributes the product's curious name not to a dialect term but to an error of transcription committed by some faceless ministerial bureaucrat, misled by the local pronunciation of the word *caciotta*, or soft cheese. Whatever the truth of the matter, it is a welcome oddity as it helps to distinguish Urbino Caciotta from Montefeltro Caciotta, which is a very similar product although it differs in the salting and maturing techniques employed. Raw, filtered milk from two milkings (70-80% ewe's milk and the rest cow's milk) is inoculated with liquid rennet. Half an hour later, the soft curd is broken up finely. It is then reheated to a temperature of 43-44°C and placed in hoops, where it is pressed with the palm of the hand to encourage draining of the whey. Salting may be either dry or in brine baths. Finally, the cheeses are matured for 15 to 30 days at a temperature of 10-14°C in rooms with 80-90% humidity. The resulting product has a mild, lingering flavour, a fatty, soft, straw-white texture and a thin yellowish outer rind. Casciotta is produced all over the province of Pesaro and excellent examples may be found at Urbino, Urbania, Mercatelli, Sant'Angelo in Vado, Pioggico, Fermignano and Caglio.

Rennet: liquid, calf's
Outer rind: fairly thin, soft and springy, beige yellow in colour.
Body: firm, straw-yellow in colour, very crumbly with a few eyes
Top and bottom: flat, round, 12-16 cm in diameter
Height/weight: 5-7 cm / 0.8 –1.2 kg
Territory of origin: the province of Pesaro
DOP status awarded on 12 June 1996, regulation no. 1107

Currently, most Casciotta d'Urbino is made from pasteurised milk but experiments have shown that raw milk will ensure superior taste characteristics.

Ewe's milk

Pecorino dei Monti Sibillini

This cheesemaking process for this Pecorino is very similar to the classic method but there are some crucial differences. About half an hour after inoculating the freshly drawn milk with rennet, the soft curd is cut up into very small pieces. It is then re-heated, unlike standard Pecorino, which is heated in the whey before maturing. The curd is transferred to hoops and pressed by hand. Then comes dry-salting, the rounds being left under salt for two days. Next comes the first part (15-20 days) of maturing, in cool rooms with medium humidity. Here, the cheeses are washed every other day with water and warm whey. Thereafter, Pecorino dei Monti Sibillini may mature for up to two years in the cellar, where it is regularly brushed with the fat that oozes out of the rind, or with olive oil.

Rennet: liquid lamb's, aromatised in various ways
Outer rind: when fresh, the rind is soft and straw-yellow. The mature version has a hard, golden yellow rind, dappled with rust-coloured patches
Body: white, firm, with few eyes
Top and bottom: flat, 14-20 cm in diameter
Height/weight: 4-9 cm / 0.8 –2.5 kg
Territory of origin: the Mountain Community of Monti Sibillini and the municipalities of Amandola and Comunanza in the province of Ascoli Piceno, and of Sarnano, Visso and Ussita in the province of Macerata

Pecorino di Montagna

To make this Pecorino, freshly drawn milk heated to a temperature of 36-37°C is inoculated with rennet in paste. After coagulation, the soft curd is broken up by hand or with a *spino* ("curd knife") into hazelnut-sized pieces for the fresh cheese, and rice-sized granules for the mature product. The curd may be reheated – *i.e.* semi-cooked - to 45-48°C, after which is transferred into moulds where it is lightly pressed by hand. When the cheese is dry, it is dry-salted by covering it completely and allowing it to absorb the salt naturally. Two days later, the cheeses go into a cool and moderately humid room, where they will remain for a minimum of 20 days. During maturing, the Pecorinos are turned over daily and washed every other day with water and warm whey.

Rennet: paste, kid's or lamb's. The rennet may be aromatised with local herbs
Outer rind: hard, firm, smooth and yellowish in colour
Body: firm, with a few eyes, and ivory or straw-white in colour
Top and bottom: flat, 15-20 cm in diameter
Height/weight: 6-10 cm / 1 –2.5 kg
Territory of origin: the mountainous areas of the Marche

Piedmont

Piedmont can point to eight DOP products and its range of varied non-DOP cheeses is also impressive. There is no corner of the region – from the mountain pastures to the valley floors, and from the low-lying Langhe to the Roero – that does not have its own ewe's milk, goat's milk or cow's milk speciality.

Bettelmatt

Bettelmatt is a particularly highly esteemed member of the Toma family of cheeses from the high pastures of the Val d'Ossola. People say that the special flavour of the valley's Tomas comes from a herb, known as *mottolina*, that grows only in Val d'Ossola. But it is the overall quality of the grazing that gives Bettelmatt its unique taste profile. Produced only in the summer months, Bettelmatt's cheesemaking technique resembles that used for Gruyère. Whole raw milk is heated to 36-40°C in copper vats and coagulated for 25-30 minutes. The soft curd is then cut into pea-sized granules, left to stand for a short time, and cooked. The curd deposits on the bottom of the vat and is then gathered up in a cloth and placed in hoops. After cooling, the curd is pressed mechanically for 12-24 hours. It then goes into brine for 10-15 days, or may be dry-salted, after which it is left in a cool place for mature for a minimum of two months.

Rennet: liquid, calf's
Outer rind: rough, brownish tending to dark brown
Body: compact, softish and oily, with faint eyes. Golden yellow or straw-yellow in colour
Top and bottom: flat, 30-40 cm in diameter
Height/weight: 10-15 cm / 5 -7 kg
Territory of origin: upper Val Formazza, in the municipality of Formazza, in the province of Novara, on the Alp of the same name on the border with Switzerland, 2,100 metres above sea level

Bra Tenero or Duro DOP

The product takes its name from the town of Bra, which was once the main centre for the maturing and sale of cheeses produced in the Cuneo Alps. Generic Bra cheese is made in the lowland dairies by coagulating usually pasteurised cow's milk from two milkings drawn in the same day, sometimes with the addition of small quantities of ewe's or goat's milk. Liquid calf's rennet is used, the milk being heated to between 27 and 32°C. The soft curd is cut with a circular movement using a Swiss-type *spino*, or curd knife, into sweetcorn-sized granules. The curd may be cut a second time just before it is placed in moulds. The rounds are pressed, then salted – usually dry-salted – for six days at twenty-four hour intervals. The Tenero, or soft, version may also be soaked in brine containing a 12% salt solution.

Rennet: liquid, calf's
Outer rind: thin, elastic and straw-white for the Tenero version, hard, robust and brown or beige for the Duro ("hard") cheese
Body: compact and elastic, with sparsely distributed eyes, ranging in colour from dirty white to straw-white for the Tenero cheese. The Duro version is firm and yellow ochre in colour
Top and bottom: flat, 30-40 cm in diameter
Height/weight: 7-9 cm / 6 -8 kg
Territory of origin: the entire province of Cuneo and the territory of the municipality of Villafranca Piemonte in the province of Turin.
DOP status awarded on 1 July 1996, regulation no. 1263

Bra d'Alpeggio DOP

The cheesemaking technique is substantially the same as that used for producing Bra in the lowlands. The main difference is that the tools used in the mountains are much less sophisticated and the procedure is almost entirely manual. The milk usually comes from Piemontese-breed cattle, kept in small or medium-sized byres and fed on local fodder. The DOP regulations also permit the addition of small quantities of ewe's or goat's milk. Milk from the evening milking, for example, is skimmed by allowing it to stand in tin-plated copper basins, which may be placed in running water. The following morning, the cream that has risen is removed with a spatula. Mountains dairies also employ a slightly higher coagulation temperature (32-35°C), produced by an open wood fire. A straw is inserted into the curd before it is cut to check that it has the desired consistency. When the straw stands up perfectly straight, the curd is ready for cutting. Before it is cut finely with a *spino*, the soft curd is diced into small cubes with a long, slender knife. It is then bundled up in a cloth and placed in a cheese mould, where it undergoes several pressing operations. These may be preceded by a rough division of the curd into sections to encourage draining of the whey. Mountain cheese presses comprise an inclined board of wood and a wooden lever, to which weights are applied. It should be remembered that Bra d'Alpeggio is only made during the summer months, from June to October, when the animals are grazed on mountain pastures.

Rennet: liquid, calf's
Outer rind: thin, elastic and straw-white for the Tenero ("soft") version; hard, robust and brown or beige for the Duro ("hard") cheese
Body: ivory white for Tenero, straw-yellow shading into ochre for Duro
Top and bottom: flat, 30-40 cm in diameter
Height/weight: 7-9 cm / 6 -8 kg
Territory of origin: municipalities in the province of Cuneo classified as "mountain" in compliance with law 25 July 1952 no. 991
DOP status awarded on 1 July 1996, regulation no. 1263

Illustrated above are Bra cheeses matured for various lengths of time. Very mature Bra was once used for grating as a substitute for Grana.

Bruss or Bross

Bruss (also known as Bross, Brussu, Bruz, Bruzzu or Buzzu) is not a real cheese so much as a normally homemade preparation to use up leftover pieces of cheese. The method of preparation varies with the cheeses used, hard cheeses, for example, having to be grated or cut into small flakes. The cheese is then carefully kneaded and put into glass or earthenware dishes. A small amount of fresh milk is added to encourage refermentation. The dishes are then put in a cool place, where they will remain until fermentation is interrupted with a measure of alcohol or a distillate, such as grappa or cognac. In areas where Robiola is produced, a fresh Robiola is cut into three pieces, which are then put into an earthenware jar with a measure of grappa or a glass of dry white wine. The jar is then left in a cool place for eight days before it is creamed by stirring the pieces twelve times. The operation is repeated on the fifteenth, twenty-eighth, thirty-fifth and forty-fifth day. The Bruss will be ready for the table after maturing for seven weeks.

Body: creamy, easy-to-spread, with a colour ranging from ivory white to straw-white
Weight: variable
Territory of origin: various zones in the region, particularly in the province of Cuneo

Cachat

A preparation based on goat's milk and goat's milk cheese, similar to Bruss but more intensely aromatised, and with better balance on the palate. Pieces of leftover, but defect-free, goat's milk cheese are mixed with freshly milked goat's milk in special glass or earthenware jars. The mixture ferments rapidly, and is stirred several times a day. After about twenty days' fermentation, juniper distillate, or in some cases a leek-based infusion, is added. The jar is then sealed and stored in a cool place.

Body: soft and easy-to-spread. Porcelain or milk white in colour.
Weight: variable
Territory of origin: Valle Stura in the province of Cuneo

Caprino di Rimella

A member of the extensive, albeit fragmentary, family of North Italian goat's milk cheeses, which cannot be identified with any specific territory with the exception of Roccaverano.

These cheeses are normally made by traditional methods, on a small scale, mainly for local consumption. That is also the case with this Tomino, produced with calf's rennet when it is to be eaten fresh or lamb's rennet, to bring out its piquancy, when it is intended for maturing. Raw goat's milk is heated to about 18-20°C, after souring naturally. A little rennet is then added and the milk is allowed to coagulate slowly. The resulting soft curd is transferred uncut to the moulds, or else cut, shaped by hand, and left to drain on hemp cloths. After three days, during which time it is dry-salted, the cheese is ready for consumption.

Rennet: liquid or paste, kid's or lamb's
Outer rind: a barely formed skin, brownish white in colour, when the cheese is fresh, light brown when mature
Body: firm, soft and easy-to-spread when fresh, brownish white in colour
Top and bottom: flat, 8-9 cm in diameter
Height/weight: 2-3 cm / 200-300 g
Territory of origin: the whole of Valsesia, especially the municipality of Rimella.

Caprino Ossolano

Once upon a time, there was a flourishing production of goat's milk cheeses in Val d'Ossola but the tradition was gradually abandoned and is now almost extinct. Recently, it has been revived, thanks to the initiative of farmer-cheesemakers originally from Lombardy. The technique employed for this Caprino Ossolano is substantially the same as for other mountain *caprinos*. Produced from March to October, it is made by allowing raw goat's milk to sour and cool to 18°C. A little rennet is then added and the milk is allowed to coagulate slowly. Next, the whole curd is put into moulds, where it is dry-salted and the whey is completely drained off. The cheese is ready for the table after it has ripened for three days.

Rennet: liquid or paste, kid's or lamb's
Outer rind: thin-skinned, creamy white or straw-yellow in colour depending on maturing
Body: soft, firm, creamy white in colour
Top and bottom: flat, 10-15 cm in diameter
Height/weight: 1-2 cm / 50-200g
Territory of origin: the municipalities of Domodossola, Varzo and Val Vigezzo

Castelmagno DOP

This blue cheese takes its name from the municipality of Castelmagno, where it has been made since ancient times. There is a document dating from 1277 stipulating an annual rent for grazing lands to be paid in kind to the Marquis of Saluzzo in Castelmagno cheeses. The product is made from the cow's milk of two consecutive milkings, to which small amounts of sheep's or goat's milk may be added. The milk is poured into copper vats, heated slightly (35-38°C), and inoculate with liquid rennet. Coagulation takes 30-90 minutes, after which the soft curd is cut into walnut-sized lumps. The whey is removed as it rises. The curd is then left hanging for 15 minutes in a dry cloth knotted at the edges before it is cut into 5-8 cm cubes. It is then bundled up again in a cloth, where it will drain for one or two days. The bundles are subsequently packed into wooden tubs to stand for three or four days. At this point, the curd is milled very finely, kneaded again with coarse salt, placed in cheese hoops and pressed. After six days, the cheeses are taken out of the moulds and dry-salted for two days by rubbing, a process that may be repeated for 20-30 days. The cheeses are then left to mature in caves. Some makers perforate their cheeses to encourage the growth of mould, in an operation reminiscent of Gorgonzola.

Rennet: liquid, calf's
Outer rind: smooth, straw-white when the cheese is young. Rough, hard and brown veined with red in colour when the product is mature
Body: semi-hard, mould-ripened. Pearly or ivory white in colour marbled with blue-green veins from maturing
Top and bottom: flat, becoming rough with maturing, 15-25 cm in diameter
Height/weight: 15-20 cm / 2 -7 kg
Territory of origin: the municipalities of Monterosso Grana, Pradleves and Castelmagno in the province of Cuneo
DOP status awarded on 1 July 1996, regulation no. 1263

Consumers today prefer white Castelmagno that has not yet developed the natural blue mould that is characteristic of the cheese when fully ripened.

Cavrin or Cevrin di Coazze

Cavrin is a cheese with outstanding potential, thanks to its freshness and fragrantly intense aromas. Unfortunately, production is in decline. Cavrin is made in the summer months from raw mixed goat's and cow's milk, or from goat's milk only, by the inoculation of calf's or lamb's rennet at a relatively low temperature (18-20°C). The process is faster than acid-only curdling but slower than rennet-based coagulation. When coagulation is complete, the soft curd is transferred into special hoops, or shaped by hand and placed on hemp cloths to drain. The top and bottom may be lightly dry-salted. The cheese is ready for the table after it has ripened for three days. Although usually eaten fresh, Cavrin may be matured for a short period of time, in which case it will take on a more intense yellow coloration and acquire a more pungent aroma.

Rennet: liquid, calf's or lamb's
Outer rind: extremely thin, almost transparent skin
Body: creamy, elastic, milk-white or straw-white in colour
Top and bottom: flat, 10-12 cm in diameter
Height/weight: 2-3 cm / 0.2 -1 kg
Territory of origin: the valley of the Sangone river in the province of Turin, especially at Cumiana, Coazze, Forno and Giaveno

Caso or Toma di Elva

The name of this cheese in the Provençal language means "homemade". The soft curd is cut twice but is not cooked, unlike Nostrale. Raw milk is heated to 30°C and liquid calf's rennet inoculated. It is left to coagulate for about one hour. The soft curd is then cut for the first time and allowed to set before it is cut up again, this time more finely into lumps about the size of a hazelnut. It is then left to ripen for three days before transfer into moulds to be pressed for two days. The rounds are then removed and salted in a brine bath for at least 24 hours. Maturing in natural environments with abundant native flora may lead to the growth of blue-green mould, reminiscent of a Castelmagno cheese. When consumed fresh, after maturing for one or two months, the flavour is similar to Bra or Nostrale.

Rennet: liquid, calf's
Outer rind: rough, developing a brown colour with maturing
Body: porcelain-white, shading into brown, sometimes dappled with bluish mould
Top and bottom: flat, 20 cm in diameter
Height/weight: 15 cm / 2-6 kg
Territory of origin: the municipality of Elva

Gorgonzola DOP

G orgonzola is blue cheese, called *erborinato* in Italian from the "parsley-green" (*erborin* in Lombard dialect) colour of the mould. Cow's milk is pasteurised and heated to 30°C before inoculation with *Penicillium roqueforti* mould, milk enzymes and liquid calf's rennet. After 25-30 minutes, the soft curd is cut, first into three to four centimetre squares. These are allowed to stand in the whey for about ten minutes before they are cut more finely into walnut-sized lumps. After being bundled into thin knotted cloths, they are drained for about half an hour. The firm curd is then transferred into perforated cylindrical moulds that are placed for about 24 hours on inclined boards, known as *spersori*, to encourage draining of the whey. Subsequently, the moulds are moved to the "purgatories", or damp (96% humidity), warm (20-22°C) ripening rooms for four or five hours. They are then drysalted. Today, high labour costs have induced some cheesemakers to use brine baths for salting instead. About one month later, the cheeses are perforated. This was once carried out with seasoned wood needles but nowadays steel or copper needles are inserted into the top and bottom of the cheese. The operation allows an even distribution of mould. "Naturally fermented" Gorgonzola, also known as *del nonno* ("Granddad's") or *antico* ("old-fashioned"), is produced in very limited quantities. It has much more conspicuous marbling, a crumblier body than normal and a much tangier flavour. The cheesemaking technique is similar, but some producers still leave the curd, which is precipitated in the evening, hanging from a stand overnight to drain and acquire the naturally occurring vein-producing mould present in the room. Another version, known as *a due paste* or "two-curd", has today almost completely disappeared. It was made by leaving the curd from the evening milking overnight and pouring onto it the milk from the following morning's milking.

Rennet: liquid, calf's
Outer rind: rough, moist, tending to a reddish colour when mature
Body: raw, compact, white or straw-white in colour marbled with blue-green from mould (veining)
Top and bottom: flat, 25-30 cm in diameter
Height/weight: 16-20 cm / 6 -13 kg
Territory of origin: in Piedmont, the provinces of Novara, Vercelli and Cuneo, and the municipality of Casale Monferrato. In Lombardy, the provinces of Bergamo, Brescia, Como, Cremona, Milan and Pavia
DOP status awarded on 12 June 1996, regulation no. 1107

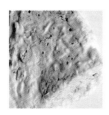

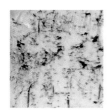

The photograph below highlights one of Gorgonzola's most popular features with today's consumers – its creaminess. The photographs on the left illustrate the difference in the body of a standard Gorgonzola and the "two body" version. The special version has more marked veining and is less moist.

Grasso d'Alpe

This cheese is the ancestor of all the mountain-produced Tomas from the valleys around Novara and Biella. The name "Grasso", or "fat", refers to the buttery texture of the body, which is redolent of rich cow's milk from high-altitude summer pastures. The milk is heated to about 30°C and inoculated with liquid calf's rennet. After 30-40 minutes, the curd is cut into pea-sized granules then left to stand for a while. It is semi-cooked at 40°C until it is completely dry. The firm curd is then allowed to deposit on the bottom of the container before it is wrapped in hemp cloths and placed in hoops. It is pressed for about 15 days and then dry-salted or salted in brine. The cheeses mature in a well-ventilated room, where they are turned over regularly and brushed or washed with water and salt. Grasso d'Alpe is ready for the table after it has matured for seventy days.

Rennet: liquid, calf's
Outer rind: smooth, medium-thick, light or mid brown in colour, depending on maturing
Body: elastic, firm, generally soft with faint eyes and a deep yellow colour
Top and bottom: flat, diameter variable from 30 to 40 cm
Height/weight: 8-15 cm / 5 -7 kg
Territory of origin: the upper part of the province of Novara, especially Val Formazza and Valle Antigorio

Mezzapasta or Spress

This cheese is a Grasso d'Alpe that has undergone prolonged maturing. The technique is distinct from that used for Grasso in that the milk is partially skimmed and the cheese is kept as dry as possible. After coagulation at a temperature of 30°C, the soft curd is cut and semi-cooked. When the curd has settled on the bottom of the cooking vessel, it is cut again. Next it is transferred into moulds, where it is vigorously pressed for several hours. The top of the round is then dry-salted, as is the bottom twenty four hours later. After salting, the cheeses are placed in well-ventilated rooms at a constant temperature of 12-15°C. Maturing lasts for three-four months but may go on for as long as 12-14 months.

Rennet: liquid, calf's
Outer rind: smooth, medium thick, light or mid brown in colour depending on maturing
Body: elastic, firm, generally soft with faint eyes and a deep yellow colour
Top and bottom: flat, 30-40 cm in diameter
Height/weight: 8-15 cm / 5 -8 kg
Territory of origin: the upper part of the province of Novara, especially Val Formazza and Valle Antigorio

Murazzano DOP

The large family of Piedmontese Robiolas includes some illustrious members, such as this Murazzano, traditionally obtained from Alta Langa ewe's milk, which was awarded DO status in 1982 and designated DOP in 1996. Today, it is increasingly difficult to find classic, pure ewe's milk Murazzano, partly because the DOP regulations permit the use of up to 40% cow's milk. Robiolas obtained from pure ewe's milk can bear the words *latte di pecora* on the label. The cheesemaking technique involves heating the milk to 37°C and inoculating it with liquid calf's rennet which has been diluted with water to assist its dispersion in the milk. Coagulation is complete after 30 minutes. The soft curd is then roughly broken up into orange-sized lumps, which are left to stand for about ten minutes. The whey that drains off is removed. The curd is then broken again into hazelnut-sized lumps and removed from the whey. After standing for a short time, the firm curd is placed in hoops. Ten minutes later, it is turned upside down for the first time, then again two hours later. One side is then dry-salted. Six or seven hours later, the cheese is turned over again and a second salting carried out. The cheeses are then placed in a lightly ventilated room on cotton cloths to absorb the whey that drains off. They ripen for seven to ten days, during which time they are turned over daily. At this stage, the Murazzano is ready for the

table but it may be left to mature for a further period of up to
two months.

Rennet: liquid, calf's
Outer rind: thin skinned, milk-white or straw-white in colour
Body: soft, firm, sometimes with faint eyes, fine-grained and straw-white in colour
Top and bottom: flat, with a slight edging, 10-15 cm in diameter
Height/weight: 3-4 cm / 300-400 g
Territory of origin: 43 municipalities in the province of Cuneo
DOP status awarded on 12 June 1996, regulation no. 1107

Genuine Murazzano DOP should be wrapped in the classic triangular paper bearing the mark of the Consortium. The cheese may present faint eyes on being sliced.

Murianengo or Moncenisio

A cheese with a strong similarity to Gorgonzola, Murianengo's origins may date back to more or less the same period as its more celebrated cousin. The earliest references to the cheese are from the eleventh century and the name derives from Val Moriana in Savoy. Some experts believe Murianengo and Moncenisio are two distinct types but the cheesemaking procedure is nearly identical. Milk, usually whole, is coagulated for 30-60 minutes. The soft curd is then cut, first into large lumps and then into hazelnut-sized pieces. It is then gathered up in a cloth and left to ferment for 24 hours in a wooden bucket. The old curd is then mixed with one half or one third of the new and the mixture is placed in moulds. It is lightly pressed, then dry-salted and the pressure is gradually increased. After 20 days, the rounds are transferred to the cellar, where they are perforated before standing for three months to allow the *Penicillium* mould to develop.

Rennet: liquid or paste, calf's
Outer rind: firm, rough and irregular, yellow shading into red in colour
Body: soft, buttery and firm, straw-white streaked with mould becoming dried and more heavily veined with maturing
Top and bottom: flat, 25-35 cm in diameter
Height/weight: 12-18 cm / 5 -12 kg
Territory of origin: the Moncenisio plateau, the southern slopes of Colle del Frejus and the Novalesa plateau

Ormea

The cheesemaking process for Ormea is very similar to that used for Bra. Whole, or partially skimmed, raw milk is heated to 30°C and inoculated with liquid calf's rennet. It is then left to coagulate. The soft curd is then cut in two stages. First, it is broken up by vigorous stirring, then by pressing. It is next transferred to moulds, where it is subjected to gradually increasing pressure for four to six hours. When the hard-pressed curd is dry, it is dry-salted with coarse salt on the top and bottom alternately for a week. At this stage, it is moved the maturing cellar. Fresh Ormea will stay there for one month but other types may remain for as long as eight months. Today, production of Ormea is in decline because cheesemakers prefer to make the better-known Raschera.

Rennet: liquid, calf's
Outer rind: thin, smooth, ranging in colour from straw-white to beige or ochre with maturing
Body: soft, firm ivory white for the soft version and dry, golden yellow or ochre for the hard
Top and bottom: flat, 25-30 cm in diameter
Height/weight: 8-12 cm / 5 -6 kg
Territory of origin: the municipalities of Ormea, Chiusa Pesio, Fontane, Frabosa Soprana, Garessio, Limone Piemonte and Pamparato in the southern part of the province of Cuneo

Paglierina

In Piedmont, the name "Paglierina" (or "Paglietta", or "D'la Paja", all meaning "straw cheese") indicates a vast range of usually fresh, flat cheeses, with or without a bloomy rind. In fact, it was the Quaglia dairy that first called one of its cheeses by this name about a century ago. Quaglia's cheese featured the distinctive marks on the surface that were once produced by the straw mats on which the product was placed to mature. The milk is coagulated at 38-40°C, then the soft curd is cut into walnut-sized lumps with a curd knife. It is then placed in moulds to drain before ripening in a damp room at 25°C for about seven hours. After dry or brine salting, the cheeses mature in a cool, damp room until a white mould forms on the surface in 10-12 days. Maturing may be extended, in which case the cheese under the rind becomes creamier as a result of proteolysis.

Rennet: liquid, calf's
Outer rind: rough, elastic, with characteristic square or lined marking; it may be covered with a bloom of white mould
Body: soft, firm and lustrous in the fresh version, firm, elastic and yellow in colour for more mature cheeses
Top and bottom: flat, 10-15 cm in diameter
Height/weight: 32 cm / 300-500 g
Territory of origin: the provinces of Cuneo and Turin

Raschera d'Alpeggio

Raschera may be called "d'Alpeggio" when it comes from zones more than 900 metres above sea level in the municipalities of Frabosa Soprana, Frabosa Sottana, Roburent, Roccaforte, Mondovì, Ormea, Garessio (only the area of Val Casotto), Magliano Alpi (the area bordering on Ormea), Montaldo and Pamparato, all in the province of Cuneo. The cheesemaking technique is substantially that described for Raschera but the mountain product offers aromas of Alpine herbs that further enhance the already outstanding taste profile of the variety. Production of the cheese, which is made in the summer months from June to the end of August, had been falling off in recent years as the Cuneo mountains became increasingly depopulated. It has now picked up again thanks to strong demand from wholesale markets and especially from restaurants.

Rennet: liquid, calf's
Outer rind: thin, reddish-grey sometimes tending to yellowish, smooth and springy
Body: soft, elastic, ivory white in colour with very few eyes
Top and bottom: flat, 35-40 cm in diameter in the cylindrical version while the quadrilateral has sides 40 cm long
Height/weight: 7-12 cm / 5 -8 kg
Territory of origin: areas more than 900 metres above sea level in some municipalities in the province of Cuneo

Cow's, ewe's and goat's milk
Raschera DOP

Raschera is the traditional cheese of the valleys around Mondovì. Its name is echoed in many of the place names in the area, such as Lake Raschera, at the foot of Monte Mongioie, the Rascaira Alp and the name attributed to the region itself, Ruscaira. Raschera is made with cow's milk, although the DOP regulations permit the addition of ewe's or goat's milk. It must come from one or two milkings drawn on the same day. It should preferably be raw, and must come from Bruno-Alpina or Piemontese cows. Liquid rennet is added to make the milk coagulate at a temperature of between 27 and 30°C in a wooden container called a *gerla*. It is then covered with a woollen cloth for about one hour, until the curd forms. When the milk has coagulated, the soft curd is cut with a special tool known as a *sbattella*. The whey is then drained off with a hemp cloth and the firm curd, now called *prod*, is placed in moulds and pressed for about ten minutes. The *prod* is then cut again and pressed for a whole day. The cylindrical rounds are then dry-salted while the quadrilateral version is pressed again for five days with a wooden mould. Raschera is matured in cool, damp rooms on wooden shelves known as *selle* for at least 20 days. Some versions are however matured for as long as three months. The outer rind is grey-brown, and may acquire reddish marks while maturing. The body is ivory-white, springy and firm, with small, irregular eyes and a strong aroma of hay and buttermilk. With maturing, the nose tends to become slightly tangy and almondy.

Rennet: liquid, calf's
Outer rind: thin, reddish-grey sometimes tending to yellowish, smooth and springy
Body: soft, elastic, ivory white in colour with very few eyes
Top and bottom: flat, 35-40 cm in diameter in the cylindrical version while the quadrilateral has sides 40 cm long
Height/weight: 7-12 cm / 5 -8 kg
Territory of origin: the province of Cuneo
DOP status awarded on 1 July 1996, regulation no. 1263

Two square Raschera cheeses with the label indicating their origin. The green label attests a Raschera from a low-lying dairy while yellow is used for Raschera d'Alpeggio.

Rebruchon

The name clearly derives from the famous Savoy cheese, Reblochon, which in the local dialect means "second milking". This particularly fat-rich milk is ideal for making creamy cheeses. On the Italian side of the mountains, a similar cheese is made, although it obvious cannot used the DOP-protected Reblochon name. The milk is filtered and heated to 35°C, then coagulated in about 30 minutes. The soft curd is then cut into walnut-sized lumps, first with a *spanarola* curd knife and then with a *lira*. After about ten minutes, the whey is drained off. The curd is then gathered up in a hemp cloth and placed in moulds, where it is lightly pressed. The rounds are removed from the moulds and placed in dry rooms, where they are dry-salted on top and bottom every other day. Brine salting is also employed. Finally, the cheeses are moved into increasingly cold rooms, where they will complete their maturation in about 20 days.

Rennet: liquid, calf's
Outer rind: thin, soft, oily, reddish yellow in colour
Body: soft, fatty, exuding droplets of whey, it may present faint eyes and is ivory white or straw-white in colour
Top and bottom: flat, 12 cm in diameter
Height/weight: 4-5 cm / 0.3 -1 kg
Territory of origin: Val Susa, especially the area of Novalesa

Robiola del Bec

The name Robiola del Bec comes from the fact that this particular cheese is traditionally made only in the months of October and November, when the she-goats are on heat and are covered by the he-goat (*bec*, *buc* or *becco* in the Piedmontese dialect). The milk has a high fat content and the cheese obtained is very creamy. Milk from the evening milking is allowed to sour. The following morning's milk is added and the mixture is brought to 18°C. A little rennet is inoculated and acid or lactic coagulation continues slowly for at least 24 hours. The soft curd is then carefully transferred to special moulds, where it remains for a day. For Robiola del Bec, the moulds are topped up as the cheese drains to obtain a higher side than for other Robiolas. Once the whey has drained off, white salt is added and the cheese is placed in a suitable room to ripen. The cheese is ready for the table after three days.

Rennet: liquid, occasionally paste, calf's
Outer rind: the fresh cheese has no skin but with maturing, acquires a rough, brown or straw-white rind that exudes droplets of whey
Body: ivory or chalk-white, firm, crumbly, soft and easy to spread
Top and bottom: flat, 12-16 cm in diameter
Height/weight: 6-8 cm / 300-600 g
Territory of origin: the entire Robiola di Roccaverano production area and the Acqui area

Robiola di Ceva or Mondovì

R obiola di Ceva or Mondovì is one of the many varieties of
Robiola produced in the province of Cuneo. It is relatively
little-known, partly because it is generally made on a very small
scale. Nevertheless, it is a cheese that deserves to be more widely
appreciated for its outstanding taste profile, thanks to the excellent quality Piemontese cow's milk that goes into it, and for the
cheesemaking technique used, which is unlike that used for other
Toma or Robiola cheeses. Coagulation takes place at a relatively
low temperature (18-22°C) over a period of at least 24 hours. The
soft curd is then gently broken up and transferred to the moulds.
After draining for about two days, the cheese is dry-salted with
white sea salt. The Robiola then completes its maturing period,
which lasts an average of 20 days. At the end of this time, the rind
will have a light bloom of white mould.

Rennet: liquid, calf's
Outer rind: soft, thin skin with a hint of bloom
Body: dry, supple and without eyes, the colour shades from ivory white to
pale straw-yellow with maturing
Top and bottom: flat, 15 cm in diameter
Height/weight: 2-3 cm / 200-350 g
Territory of origin: the entire Upper Val Tanaro

Robiola di Roccaverano DOP

Robiola di Roccaverano can be made with raw or pasteurised milk but in the latter case, milk enzymes are used as well as rennet. Milk from two daily milkings is heated to 18°C and inoculated with liquid calf's rennet or else, rarely but in accordance with ancient custom, with kid's rennet in paste. It is left to coagulate for 24 hours and then the unbroken curd is placed in plastic hoops for a further day. The product is now salted and left to ripen for three days in rooms with a controlled temperature of between 15 and 20°C. The cheese will then be ready for the table but it is often left to mature for a further 20 days, especially when it contains a high proportion of kid's milk. The current DOP regulations permit the use of up to 85% cow's milk, mixed with varying proportions of ewe's and goat's milk. However, cheesemakers are campaigning for a modification of the rules that would promote Robiola di Roccaverano made in the traditional manner, without cow's milk. If their request is granted, this Robiola will have the adjective *classica* added to its designation and will be produced with pure goat's milk, or goat's milk mixed with a small amount of ewe's milk. Robiola di Roccaverano is made in the territory of two Piedmontese provinces, Bobbio, Cessole, Loazzolo, Mombaldone, Monastero Bormida, Olmo Gentile, Roccaverano, San Giorgio Scarampi, Serole and Vesime in the province of Asti; and Castelletto d'Erro, Denice,

Malvicino, Merana, Montechiaro d'Acqui, Pareto, Ponti, Spigno and part of the municipality of Cartosio in the province of Alessandria.

Rennet: liquid, calf's
Outer rind: very thin skinned, ivory-white in colour, tending to straw-yellow or brownish with reddish streaks after maturing
Body: fresh, tender and firm, white
Top and bottom: flat, with a slight edging, 10-14 cm in diameter
Height/weight: 4-5 cm / 400 g
Territory of origin: part of the provinces of Asti and Alessandria
DOP status awarded on 1 July 1996, regulation no. 1263

This is the only goat's milk cheese in Italy to enjoy DOP status, bearing witness to the ancient origins of goat's milk cheesemaking in this part of Piedmont.

Seirass del Fen

The name *Seirass*, *Seras* or *Seré* derives from the Latin *Seracium* and is the local name for Ricotta in Piedmont and Valle d'Aosta. The product has many different forms in the region, ranging from rounded cones to cylinders or an upturned basket-shape. When dried and salted, it may have a roundish shape and varies in weight. The cheesemaking technique is the classic Ricotta method - the whey is heated to 90°C – with the difference that Seirass del Fen whey comes from mountain dairy milk used to make Toma cheese. As is well-known, the whey of soft cheeses produces soft Ricottas while whey from cooked cheeses gives a more solid product. It is also difficult to obtain ricotta from pasteurised milk naturally. After 12-36 hours, the Seirass is taken out of its moulds or cloths and kneaded by hand with white salt. It is then exposed to the atmosphere. This operation is repeated several times. The cheeses are then placed in a dry, well-ventilated room to dry, after which they are wrapped in freshly cut hay (*fieno* or *fen*). In some cases, the Seirass is also lightly smoked.

Body: the fresh cheese has a delicate, lumpy body while the mature version has a firm, translucent, brownish-white or straw-white body.
Height/weight: varying from 2-5 kg
Territory of origin: Seirass is made almost everywhere in Piedmont but hay maturing is typical of the valleys around Pinerolo

Söra, Sola or Soela

Söra is a typical mountain cheese, which is especially good in summer. Its origins are lost in the mists of time and it is mentioned by the historian, Tullio Pagliana, in a study of the lives of shepherds in the Upper Val Tanaro. The name derives from the dialect term that indicates the sole of a shoe because of its characteristic flat, square shape. The cheese itself is made with raw milk heated to 30-36°C and coagulated with liquid rennet. After the soft curd is broken up, it is wrapped in a cloth to drain the whey. When dry, it is kneaded and then placed in moulds before being pressed. The subsequent stages involve dry-salting and then maturing, which takes place in fairly dry cellars at a temperature of 10°C.

Rennet: liquid, calf's
Outer rind: vestigial, straw-yellow in colour, thickening with maturing and shading into brown
Body: soft, lustrous, firm, with faint eyes, cream in colour tending to ivory or yellow when mature
Top and bottom: flat, 15-25 cm in diameter
Height/weight: 3-4 cm / 2 -4 kg
Territory of origin: mountain pastures at the head of the Tanaro river valley in the territory of the municipality of Ormea, in Valcasotto and in the valleys around Mondovì

Testun

The technique for making this classic mountain Toma cheese is very similar to that employed for Bra. It differs in that only ewe's milk is used, or else ewe's milk mixed with small quantities of cow's milk. Testun, which in the Piedmontese dialect means a "big, hard head", had almost completely disappeared from the market. But now its extraordinary taste profile has earned it a reprieve. The milk is coagulated at 37°C and the soft curd is cut into hazelnut-sized pieces. It is then left to stand in whey for about an hour, after which it is wrapped up, kneaded and placed in moulds, where it is pressed. After pressing, the rounds are dry-salted on top and bottom alternately with sea salt. They are then placed in cellars or caves to mature for a period ranging from two to twelve months or even longer. Once, very mature Testun was also used for grating.

Rennet: liquid, calf's
Outer rind: thin, yellow-brown in colour, often scored with marks left by the rush mats used for maturing
Body: firm, brownish-white or straw-white in colour; extended maturing may result in traces of marbling
Top and bottom: flat, sometimes with slight roughness, 30-36 cm in diameter
Height/weight: 8-10 cm / 4 -8 kg
Territory of origin: the province of Cuneo between the river Tanaro and the torrential river Vermenagna, exclusively in mountain dairies

Toma del Bot

Toma cheeses are made from ewe's milk in Valle Stura under the name of Toma Valle Stura, or from cow's milk, in which case they are sold as Toma del Bot. Whole raw milk is heated to 37°C, and then coagulated with liquid calf's rennet for two hours. The soft curd is then broken up with a tool called a *bourcet* and allowed to settle on the bottom of the vat. Afterwards, a perforated cloth called a *reirola* is used to remove and press it before it is kneaded and shaped. The pressed curd is left so that the remaining whey can drain off and then top and bottom are dry-salted for a period of at least 24 hours. The Toma del Bot is then cellared to mature for three months, during which time the cheeses are regularly turned over and, if necessary, moistened with brine.

Rennet: liquid, calf's
Outer rind: thick, rough, varying in colour from straw-yellow to brown, depending on the maturing period
Body: soft, firm, straw-white or golden yellow in colour
Top and bottom: flat, 10-15 cm in diameter
Height/weight: 5 cm / 3-10 kg
Territory of origin: the Upper Valle Stura in the province of Cuneo

COW'S MILK

Toma del Maccagno

Maccagno is one of the finest Tomas to be found in the mountains of Biella and Vercelli. It takes its name from the Maccagno Alp, which lies in below Monte Cossarello north of Biella, and was the favourite cheese of Queen Margherita of Savoy. Mountain Toma is made by heating raw milk – in the past, shepherds used to filter it first through a layer of ferns or nettles – to 37°C and inoculating liquid calf's rennet. After about two hours, the curd is broken up into lumps three to eight millimetres across and left to settle on the bottom of the vat. The whey is then removed and the curd is wrapped in a perforated cloth before being placed in cheese hoops. The rounds stand for two hours, and are turned over repeatedly. Salting, today usually carried out in brine baths, is the next stage, after which the rounds are washed and then placed in maturing rooms. The maturing process lasts for four weeks, during which time the cheeses are regularly turned over and washed with brine.

Rennet: liquid, calf's
Outer rind: thin, smooth, brown in colour, tending to reddish
Body: firm, elastic, with faint eyes, varying in colour from straw-white to golden yellow
Top and bottom: flat, 10-15 cm in diameter
Height/weight: 8-10 cm / 3 -4 kg
Territory of origin: the Biella area, in particular the Cervo, Elvo and Sessera valleys

PIEDMONT

195

Toma di Balme

The classic mountain cheesemaking technique is used to make Toma di Balme. If whole milk from a single milking is used, the cheese is not semi-cooked. The milk is heated to 37°C, inoculated with liquid calf's rennet and allowed to coagulate. The soft curd is then broken with a curd knife known locally as a *bourceret* into lumps the size of walnuts. It is allowed to settle and then removed using a perforated cloth called a *reirola*. Once drained, the curd is hand-kneaded and moulded roughly into shape. It is then placed on a special shelf called an *iloira*, where it remains for 24 hours until the whey has completely drained. Next, the tops and bottoms of the rounds are dry-salted for a further 24 hours. In the past, some cheesemakers also sprinkled pepper on their products. At this point, the cheeses are placed in a damp room, where they mature for an average of one month.

Rennet: liquid, calf's
Outer rind: smooth, thin and straw or golden yellow when fresh, thick, rough and dark brown in colour when mature
Body: firm, elastic, liberally scattered with eyes, deep yellow in colour
Top and bottom: flat, 20-40 cm in diameter
Height/weight: 8-15 cm / 3 -11 kg
Territory of origin: some mountain dairies in the municipality of Balme (the Cumba and Pian Gioé Giasset dairies)

Toma di Lanzo

This Toma is one of the territory-specific products that have never been included in the extensive family of the Toma Piemontese DOP. Its main distinguishing characteristics are its less regular shape and the pastures where the milk for the summer version comes from. After heating to 37°C, the milk is inoculated with liquid rennet and left to coagulate. The time required will depend on the milk's fat content and the rennet used. Next, the soft curd is cut roughly and left to drain before a second cutting is performed to produce sweetcorn-sized granules. It is left to settle for five minutes and then transferred to cheese hoops, where it is pressed for two days. Dry-salting, which takes a week, is the next stage. Many cheesemakers still add salt to the curd when it is removed from the vat. The rounds are then placed in natural caves, where they ripen for one month and mature for at least three. During this time, the cheese are turned over every day.

Rennet: liquid, calf's
Outer rind: smooth, medium-hard, brown or dark brown in colour
Body: firm, fairly hard during maturing, brownish-white or straw-white in colour
Top and bottom: flat, 30-35 cm in diameter
Height/weight: 10 cm / 4-8 kg
Territory of origin: Valle di Lanzo, particularly Val Grande and Valle di Ala

Toma or Robiola d'Alba

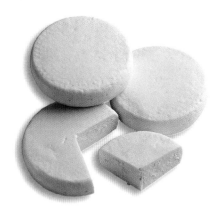

The name "Robiola" is believed to come from Robbio Lomellina, a municipality where this kind of cheese has been made since time immemorial, or else from the Latin *ruber* (meaning "red"), and its derivative *rubeola*, from the colour of the cheese's skin after maturing. In the province of Cuneo, the word "Toma" is used for this cheese, although this is not strictly accurate because the term generally refers to large Alpine cheeses. Cheese-making techniques, too, may vary considerably from area to area. Usually, cow's milk from a single milking is first coagulated at a temperature of 35-38°C. The soft curd is then broken up into hazelnut-sized lumps and then transferred to moulds, where is stands for about eight hours at a temperature of 18-25°C. This is called "pre-maturing". The next stage is dry-salting before the cheese goes into a cool, damp room for up to eight days, in the case of the fresh version, or 40-50 days for the mature. Traditional Toma d'Alba has a firm body that breaks cleanly when cut.

Rennet: liquid, calf's
Outer rind: white or faintly straw-coloured skin in the fresh version, grey-brown with reddish tones in mature cheeses.
Body: buttery, soft, almost entirely free of eyes; cream in colour, shading into translucent straw-white with maturing
Top and bottom: flat, 10-20 cm in diameter
Height/weight: 2-4 cm / 200-400 g
Territory of origin: the whole of Valsesia, especially the province of Cuneo.

Toma Piemontese DOP

There is still debate about the origin of the word "Toma", which is widely used in Piedmont, Valle d'Aosta, France, Savoy, the Pyrenees and even in Sicily. One of the possible explanations is that it refers to the precipitation of casein during coagulation as the dialect word for "fall" is *tomé*. But within the great family of Toma cheeses, Toma Piemontese is one of the most quantitatively significant and the only one so far to enjoy DOP status. Milk from two consecutive milkings (or one only, if whole milk is used) is left to stand for up to 12 hours if a whole milk product is desired or 24 for the semi-fat cheese made from milk skimmed after the cream has been allowed to rise. The milk is then put in a cheese vat, stirred gently and heated to 32-35°C before inoculation with calf's rennet. Forty minutes later, the curd is broken, and may also be reheated in a sort of semi-cooking process, until rice-sized granules settle on the bottom of the vat. The curd is then removed and placed in hoops where it is pressed, turned over and dry-salted with coarse salt on top and bottom for up to 15 days. Otherwise, the rounds may be salted in a brine bath for a period of between 24 and 48 hours. The cheeses are then matured, usually in natural environments but also in special rooms where they are regularly turned over and brushed or washed with brine from time to time. Maturing lasts for at least 60 days for cheeses weighing over six kilograms and 15 days for lighter cheeses. Toma Piemontese is produced nearly everywhere in Piedmont, especially in the hinterland of the provinces of Novara, Vercelli, Biella, Turin and Cuneo, in the municipalities of Acqui Terme, Terzo, Bistagno, Ponti and Denice in the province of Alessandria, and in the municipalities of Monastero Bormida, Roccaverano, Mombaldone, Olmo Gentile and Serole in the province of Asti.

Rennet: liquid or paste, calf's
Outer rind: smooth, elastic, varying in colour from straw-white to reddish brown
Body: firm, springy, may present faint eyes.
Top and bottom: flat, 15-35 cm in diameter
Height/weight: 5-12 cm / 2 -8 kg
Territory of origin: the provinces of Novara, Vercelli, Biella, Turin and Cuneo as well as some municipalities in the provinces of Alessandria and Asti
DOP status awarded on 1 July 1996, regulation no. 1263

Toma Piemontese DOP – the label can be seen in the illustration - embraces an astonishing range of Piedmont mountain Toma cheese that differ in shape, weight and maturing.

Tomino di Talucco

The traditional technique used to make this cheese begins with the heating of pure goat's milk to a temperature of about 85°C. When the milk has cooled to 38°C, it is inoculated with liquid calf's rennet and left to coagulate for 40 minutes. Next, the soft curd is carefully cut into largish lumps and then poured into moulds. A day later, top and bottom are dry-salted, although some cheesemakers salt the milk itself. The next day, the Tomino is ready for to be consumed fresh. But the tradition method includes maturing. Once hard, the Tominos are placed in earthenware *ule*, or jars and sprinkled with black pepper or garden thyme and wild thyme.

Rennet: liquid, calf's
Outer rind: no rind when fresh. Thin, hard and reddish yellow when mature
Body: fine-grained, soft and moist. Chalk-white tending to brownish white with maturing
Top and bottom: flat, 5 cm in diameter
Height/weight: 32 cm / 50-500 g
Territory of origin: the villages of Grandubbione and Talucco in Val Chisone

Toumin del Mel

Toumin was created in the mid-nineteenth century on the slopes of Valle Varaita, later taking its name from the municipality of Melle, or Mel, where it was sold. The cheese is made by adding a little rennet to whole, freshly drawn milk and leaving the curd to stand at room temperature for a fairly long period of time that varies depending on the individual cheesemaker's style. Subsequently, the curd is cut into large lumps and then transferred into the traditional moulds with a skimming spoon. The moulds are turned over several times, salted on top and bottom, and placed in a cool, damp place to mature. Toumin releases fresh, tangy aromas of buttermilk and yoghurt, with nuances of fresh hay that are transformed into mossy notes with maturing. On the palate, it is mild, full-flavoured and faintly sourish. In its territory of origin, Toumin is used as a filling for the traditional Valle Varaita *ravioles*. With maturing, the nose tends to become slightly tangy and almondy.

Rennet: liquid, calf's
Outer rind: when fresh, Toumin has a milky white skin that becomes porcelain white with maturing
Body: fatty, raw, soft. Milky white in colour, with no eyes
Top and bottom: flat, 10-12 cm in diameter
Height/weight: 1-2 cm / 150-200 g
Territory of origin: the municipalities of Melle, Frassino and Valmala in Valle Varaita

Valcasotto

This outstanding mountain dairy cheese, now almost impossible to find, is made with whole raw cow's milk to which small quantities of ewe's milk, or very occasionally goat's milk, have been added. The milk is heated to 38°C and inoculated with liquid calf's rennet. After it has coagulated fairly slowly, the curd is cut into walnut-sized lumps and then removed. It is ripened in a warm, damp room at a temperature of 26°C for a few hours. The firm curd is then placed in moulds, where the remaining whey is drained off. The next stages are salting in brine and maturing for 10 to 20 days at a temperature of about 5°C. Extended maturing produces a creamy body and a thicker rind that dramatically alter the cheese's taste profile.

Rennet: liquid, calf's
Outer rind: there is almost no rind when the cheese is fresh. Rough and brown, streaked with reddish mould when very mature
Body: soft, ivory-white or straw-white in colour
Top and bottom: flat, 15-25 cm in diameter
Height/weight: 2-4 cm / 0.3 -1 kg
Territory of origin: Upper Valle Tanaro, in mountain dairies on the border between Piedmont and Liguria

Puglia

Puglia's flagship cheese is Cacioricotta, a speciality that combines in a single product the characteristics of both Ricotta and goat's milk cheese. The region is also the home of many other excellent cheeses, including Burrata, Canestrato, and Podolico del Gargano.

Burrata

The method used to make Burrata is very similar to that used for Mozzarella, differing only in the stretching technique employed and, of course, the fact that Burrata has a filling. The main difference lies in the method used to form the "bag". A layer of stretched-curd about one centimetre thick is moulded and formed into the desired envelope shape. The bag is then filled with strings of stretchy curd that have been amalgamated with cream from the whey, obtained by separating leftover whey from Mozzarella production in a centrifuge. The bags are knotted at the neck while still warm, as they lie in the water where the curd was stretched. The Burrata is then dipped in brine for a few minutes to salt it. After salting, the cheeses are packed into bags, plastic tubs or film, and are then ready to go on sale. When it reaches the table, Burrata is smooth on the outside, lustrous white in colour, and has a mild, buttery taste.

Rennet: liquid, calf's
Body: composite, comprising a plastic cheese envelope filled with cream of whey
Top and bottom: smooth, 10-20 cm in diameter
Weight: 0.5-1 kg
Territory of origin: the municipalities of Andria and Martina Franca

Caciofiore

Caciofiore does not have an established tradition behind it as it has only been produced for the last 30 years or so. To make it, pasteurised ewe's milk is inoculated with rennet and a starter culture. The soft curd obtained is broken up, worked together in the bottom of the cheese vat, shaped and, on the following day, salted in a brine bath. Its outer rind is very thin while the body of the cheese is soft and has a sweetish, buttery smell. Caciofiore is allowed to ripen for a short time and is marketed as a table cheese.

Rennet: liquid, calf's
Outer rind: smooth or wrinkled, straw-white in colour
Body: uncooked, soft, ivory-white or creamy white in colour
Top and bottom: flat, varying in diameter
Height/weight: 3-4 cm / 0.4-1.5 kg
Territory of origin: the entire province of Foggia

Cacioricotta

Cacioricotta, one of the best known southern Italian cheeses, is made in Puglia, Basilicata and Cilento. It probably takes its name from the method employed to make it, which involves heating the milk to a temperature of 85-90°C and then cooling it to about 37°C. This a process that causes the milk to coagulate, as in the Cacio cheesemaking process, and the proteins in the whey to precipitate, which is how Ricotta is obtained. The resulting curd is poured into rush baskets and salted the day after it is made. Cacioricotta is ivory-white in colour and soft in texture when fresh, becoming golden yellow, hard and firm with a tangy flavour after maturing. It is similar to Ricotta in appearance. Cacioricotta can be eaten fresh with starters or main courses while the mature version is used for grating.

Rennet: paste, lamb's or kid's
Outer rind: lined, brownish white in colour
Body: uncooked, soft or hard, firm and free of eyes. Brownish-white in colour
Top and bottom: flat, 13-20 cm in diameter
Height/weight: 6-9 cm / 0.5-2 kg
Territory of origin: the entire region

Canestrato Pugliese DOP

Canestrato Pugliese is a fundamental part of the cheesemaking heritage in Puglia, being closely bound up with the traditional movement of flocks to summer pastures that was practised right up to the end of the 1950s. The DOP territory covers the entire province of Foggia and the municipalities of Canosa, Cassano, Altamura, Minervino, Ruvo di Puglia, Bitonto, Andria, Murge, Terlizzi, Toritto, Poggiorsini, Grumo Appuale, Coroto, Gravina di Puglia, Santeramo and Spinazzola. The raw milk from two milkings, drawn from sheep fed with fodder grown in the DOP zone, is heated to a temperature of 37°C and inoculated with liquid rennet. After about 20 minutes, the soft curd is broken and then usually semi-cooked at a temperature of 42°C. It is put in rush baskets, pressed by hand, cooked in boiling whey and dry-salted on the following day by sprinkling it with coarse sea salt. Canestrato Pugliese can be aged for up to 10 months on wooden boards placed in caves or cool, dry cellars. During the ageing process, the outer rind is treated with olive oil and, in some cases, with wine vinegar. Gold in colour on the outside, it is straw-yellow inside. The body is firm in texture with small eyes and has a fairly tangy taste. Canestrato Pugliese is used predominantly for grating over a variety of first courses, including *orecchiette, capunti,* and other traditional types of pasta from the region, and is also an ingredient in a range of typical regional dishes, including artichokes, *lampascioni in umido* (stewed small, bitterish onions), stuffed rolls of lamb and many others.

Rennet: liquid, calf's or lamb's
Outer rind: firm-textured, hard and wrinkled. Yellow or brown in colour
Body: crumbly and hard, with very fine eyes. Straw-yellow shading into bright yellow in colour
Top and bottom: flat, 14-34 cm in diameter
Height/weight: 10-14 cm / 2-14 kg
Territory of origin: the entire province of Foggia and many other bordering municipalities
DOP status awarded on 12 June 1996, regulation no. 1107

Canestrato Pugliese takes it name from the traditional practice of shaping the cheese in rush baskets. These "canestri" are responsible for the marks on the outer rind.

Fallone di Gravina

In the local dialect, the term *fallone* means a worthless, insignificant person. So Fallone, an extremely good fresh cheese, may owe its name to the fact that it lasts only a very short time and has to be eaten on the day it is made. Shepherds and cheesemakers have been using raw milk to make Fallone for centuries but small-scale producers today have adopted pasteurised milk. Nevertheless, they continue to use the mixture of ewe's milk with 10-15% goat's milk that gives Fallone its slightly tangy taste. When the milk has been heated up to about 40°C, it is inoculated with rennet. The rennet should, if possible, be at least one year old and is dissolved in tepid water before going into the milk. After about 15 minutes, the soft curd is broken into small pieces, separated from the whey, and pressed firmly by hand. It is then divided into lumps of the required size and placed in moulds that used to be made of rushes but are now plastic. At Gravina, Fallone is made by all the small local dairies but only to order, as it deteriorates so quickly.

Rennet: liquid, calf's
Body: white, soft, fatty and firm
Top and bottom: flat, 15-20 cm in diameter
Height/weight: 10 cm / 0.5-2 kg
Territory of origin: Gravina di Puglia and the surrounding area

Fior di Latte

A milk or whey-based starter culture is added to pasteurised cow's milk. This is followed by liquid calf's rennet. The soft curd is broken, left to drain and, when adjudged ready for stretching, it is cut and worked. Fior di Latte is usually salted in a brine bath. White in colour, it has an elastic texture and may either be eaten as a table cheese or used as an ingredient for cooking, especially in pizzas. The designation "Fior di Latte", which means "top of the milk", is used to differentiate Mozzarella made with buffalo's milk from cow's milk Mozzarella.

Rennet: liquid, calf's
Outer rind: there is a very fine skin
Body: plastic, soft and moist. Creamy white in colour
Top and bottom: smooth and round
Height/weight: variable / 50-500 g
Territory of origin: the entire region

COW'S MILK

Podolico del Gargano

The milk is heated in a cheese vat to a temperature of 37°C and coagulated with liquid calf's rennet or a paste of kid's rennet. After about half an hour, the soft curd is broken into granules, then worked back together into a lump and left to drain. Part of the whey is removed, heated to make the ricotta, and added to the curd, which in the meantime has been broken up and heated to at a temperature of 60-65°C to encourage it to ripen. This process is repeated two or three times. After a few hours, the curd is cut and moulded into a Caciocavallo shape. The pressed curds are salted in a brine bath for 24-48 hours and left to age in cellars. Very mature Podolico del Gargano is a much sought-after delicacy. Its deep straw-yellow body is hard in texture and has a very tangy flavour. At table, Podolico del Gargano is an especially satisfying when served with full-bodied red wines.

Rennet: liquid lamb's, or paste kid's
Outer rind: smooth and fine, tending to thicken as the cheese ages
Body: plastic, uncooked and firm with very few eyes. The body of the semi-mature cheese is elastic, becoming hard and crumbly in the mature version
Top and bottom: smooth, 15 cm at its widest diameter
Height/weight: 30 cm / 1.5-2.5 kg
Territory of origin: all over the Gargano are in the province of Foggia

Ricotta Forte

Ricotta Forte is made by heating whey obtained from ewe's or cow's milk to a temperature of 90°C. Sometimes, a small amount of ewe's or cow's milk is added to the whey. The proteins rise to the surface, where they are left to solidify for a short time, and then strained off to be put into moulds. The solids are left for a few days to gain acidity then transferred to terracotta containers, where they are kneaded every two or three days for three to four months in a cool, damp environment. This version of Ricotta is a dark ivory in colour and has a tangy flavour. It is used predominantly in pasta dishes, such as the meat sauce-based *cavatelli al ragù*. It may also be eaten spread on toasted bread.

Body: fatty, moist and creamy, brownish-white in colour
Height/weight: variable
Territory of origin: the province of Lecce and some areas in the provinces of Brindisi, Taranto and Bari

Scamorza

Rennet is inoculated into ewe's milk to coagulate it and the soft curd is broken down into small pieces before being re-heated to a temperature of 40-45°C for 10-15 minutes. After about 24 hours, when the curd has ripened sufficiently, it is stretched and moulded. The future Scamorza cheeses are then cooled in cold water and put in a brine bath for a period that varies according to the weight of the individual cheese. Scamorza can be eaten fresh or it may be aged for a short time. The mature cheese has a fine outer rind and a less elastic, more solid body. It can be used for grating or as an ingredient in a typical traditional local dish called *quagghiaridde*, or in a wide range of vegetable-based recipes.

Rennet: liquid, calf's
Outer rind: smooth, thin skin. Brownish-white or straw-white in colour
Body: plastic, elastic or solid. Semi-cooked, buttery in texture and without eyes. Ivory-white in colour
Top and bottom: smooth, 10-16 cm high
Height/weight: 6-12 cm / 300-700 g
Territory of origin: the entire province of Bari

Sardinia

Sardinia is sheep country. There are more than seven million of them in a region that has been making cheese since time immemorial. Pecorino, or ewe's milk cheese, is the main product and comes in all shapes, sizes and stages of maturity, from fresh to soft, from Caciotta al Fiore Sardo to Casu Marzu and Pecorino Romano.

Bonassai

B onassai was developed by the Bonassai Institute of Animal Husbandry and Cheesemaking, whose production methods are so well established they are now considered traditional. Pasteurised milk is inoculated with a starter culture and coagulation is complete in about 30 minutes. The soft curd is first broken up roughly with a *lira* curd knife, then reduced to walnut-sized nuggets with a *spanarola*. After this, it is poured, still in its whey, into moulds. The cheeses are placed in a warm room, where the temperature encourages draining, and are turned over regularly. When they have dried out, the cheeses are salted in a brine bath and left to mature for 20-30 days in a very damp, cool place.

Rennet: liquid, calf's
Outer rind: thin, wrinkled, straw-white in colour
Body: soft, fatty, milk or ivory-white in colour
Top and bottom: flat, 18 cm along each side when square, 9 by 18 cm in the rectangular version
Height/weight: 5-6 cm / 2-2.5 kg
Territory of origin: a number of municipalities in the provinces of Nuoro, Sassari and Cagliari

Callu de Cabreddu

Callu de Cabreddu is still made according to the traditional methods once used by the prehistoric pastoral tribes that originally inhabited the island. When a kid is butchered, its fourth stomach, or "vell", is emptied, cleaned thoroughly, filled with raw milk and hung up to mature *su cannittu* ("on reed stands") in a cool place. The cheese is then aged, a process that lasts until the skin of the stomachs stiffens to an almost board-like hardness, usually after at least four months. During ageing, Callu de Cabreddu is smoked so that the fumes from the outside and the natural enzymes in the milk combine to encourage coagulation, producing a creamy cheese with a tangy taste and a pungent smell. Callu de Cabreddu is eaten fresh as a spread may also be used on canapés as a starter.

Rennet: natural, present in the fourth stomachs of kids
Outer rind: the vell, or dried kid's stomach
Body: uncooked, soft, grey-white in colour
Top and bottom: flat, 12-18 cm in diameter
Height/weight: variable
Territory of origin: the central part of the island, in the provinces of Oristano, Nuoro and Cagliari

Caprino a Latte Crudo

R aw milk is heated directly over a flame to a temperature of 36°C and coagulated by inoculation with kid's rennet that has been diluted with water and filtered. The soft curd is broken either by hand or with a wooden curd knife and the granules are left to settle on the bottom of the vat. Following this, the curd is divided into lumps, put into moulds, salted in brine and then placed on a *canniciato* ("rush rack") and smoked over a holm-oak wood fire. The outer rind is yellow or brown while the body of the cheese is firm and white or straw-yellow. It is tangy in flavour, depending on the length of time it has been aged in the underground cellars used for this purpose. Caprino a Latte Crudo can be eaten as a table cheese or used as an ingredient in a wide variety of recipes.

Rennet: kid's, diluted in water
Outer rind: firm, varying in hardness. Yellow or brownish-yellow in colour
Body: uncooked and hard. Ivory-white or pale straw-white in colour
Top and bottom: flat, 20-30 cm in diameter
Height/weight: 12-18 cm / 1.5-3.5 kg
Territory of origin: the entire region

Casu Axedu

The milk is heated to a temperature of 35-36°C, inoculated with whey from the previous day's cheesemaking, and coagulated with kid's rennet. After about 30 minutes, the soft curd is broken into rectangles and left to drain overnight. The next day the curd is shaped and will be ready for the table only a few hours later. Casa Axedu has a slightly acidic taste. Sometimes, it is left to drain for 48 hours then steeped in very salty brine where it can be conserved for a long time. If it has undergone this treatment, the cheese is called *fiscidu* and is used as an ingredient in various local soups or as a filling for the area's traditional potato ravioli.

Rennet: paste, kid's
Body: uncooked, soft and slightly acidic. White or straw-white in colour
Top and bottom: rectangular, flat
Height/weight: 4-7 cm / 150-300 g
Territory of origin: almost the entire region

Casu Marzu

Casa Marzu is produced seasonally throughout the region, particularly in the province of Nuoro. The basis of this product is Pecorino cheese, mainly Fiore Sardo, that has gone off because of infestation by the maggots of the cheese fly, *Piophila casei*, a process actively encouraged by the cheesemaker. As the maggots eat their way through the body of the cheese, it turns into an extremely tangy, aromatic cream. Casu Marzu can be kept for a maximum of four months, after which it develops an unpleasant smell and taste. It is an uncooked cheese, obtained by a combined proteolytic and lipolytic ageing process, and has a creamy body that varies in colour from yellow to brown and a distinctly tangy flavour.

Body: uncooked and creamy. Varying from yellow to brown in colour
Territory of origin: the whole region, especially the province of Nuoro

Fiore Sardo DOP

Fiore Sardo can be manufactured industrially with a mixture of pasteurised, or occasionally raw, ewe's and cow's milk but traditionally this cheese is made exclusively from freshly drawn, raw ewe's milk. Native Sardinian sheep are believed to be descended directly from the wild mountain sheep that today still inhabit the most inaccessible parts of the island and the origins of this cheese go far back in time, possibly even to the Bronze Age Nuraghe period. Production is authorised throughout the whole region of Sardinia but traditionally Fiore Sardo is made by mountain shepherds in the huts, known as *pinnette*, whose central open fires give the authentic version its characteristically smoky overtones. Today, Sardinian shepherds still make the cheese in the time-honoured fashion. Milk from one milking is poured untreated into a cheese vat – once, a wooden tub was used and the vat is the only concession to modern technology – and coagulated with a paste of kid's or lamb's rennet. The soft curd is broken with a curd knife called a *chiova*, left to drain, and then cut with a *sa sega casu*, or "cheese saw". The now firm curd is shaped in moulds, officially described as "two truncated cones joined at their wider base", whose diameter is inferior to the diameter of the cheese in the centre. The moulds are immersed in hot water, so that the outer rind thickens, and then salted in a brine bath. After salting, Fiore Sardo is left to age, first in the *pinetta* where it was made on a rush trellis suspended over the fireplace, then on a platform under the roof of the dairy, and finally in underground cellars where the cheeses are periodically turned over and greased with olive oil, which may be mixed with sheep fat. The ageing process lasts for a total of two to eight months.

Rennet: paste, lamb's or kid's
Outer rind: dry and hard. Varying in colour from intense yellow to deep brown shading into black
Body: firm textured, straw-yellow or white in colour and with no eyes. The hardness varies according to the maturing period
Top and bottom: flat, 12-25 cm in diameter
Height/weight: 13-15 cm / 1-5 kg
DOP status awarded on 1 July 1996, regulation no. 1263

If aged for a long time, the body of Fiore Sardo tends to become rock hard and crumbly, making it ideal for grating.

Fresa

Fresa is a very similar cheese to Stracchino in character. The milk is heated to a temperature of 36-37°C and coagulated in 30-40 minutes by adding calf's rennet. The soft curd is broken by hand into fairly large pieces and allowed to drain, before being gathered up and put into moulds. The rounds are then either dry-salted or salted in a brine bath. The outer rind is yellowish while the body has a deep straw-yellow colour and a slightly acidic taste. Fresa is one of Sardinia's very few soft cheeses and can be eaten either fresh or fried. There is also a version made with ewe's milk.

Rennet: liquid, calf's
Outer rind: thin, very pale straw-white in colour
Body: uncooked and moist. Straw-yellow in colour
Top and bottom: flat
Height/weight: 5 cm / 1-1.5 kg
Territory of origin: the municipalities of Bonoria, Bortigali, Bosa, Macomer, and Silanus

Gioddu

Legend has it that a shepherd from central Sardinia left a cork bucket full of freshly drawn ewe's milk in the corner of a pen and forgot all about it. The following day, he tasted the milk before throwing it away and found that it was rather good. This was the birth of the Mizzurado ("improved") or Gioddu cheese that today is made by heating ewe's milk to a temperature of 80-95°C, then cooling it down to 45°C. In former times, red-hot stones were put into the milk to heat it. When it has reached the required temperature, a starter culture is added. The ingredients are a secret closely guarded by each family that makes Gioddu, although the basic culture is the same as that used to make yoghurt. After the desired level of coagulation has been reached, the soft curd is broken up and at this point, Gioddu is ready for the table. However, it may also be left to ripen for a few days.

Rennet: milk-enzyme starter culture
Body: grainy and almost liquid in consistency. Creamy white in colour
Territory of origin: the entire region

Ircano

The cheesemaking technique for Ircano involves pasteurising milk by heating it to 72°C and keeping it at this temperature for 15-30 minutes. It is then cooled down to 36-38°C and a starter culture of milk enzymes is added, to be followed immediately by rennet. When the soft curd has reached the required consistency, about 30 minutes after the rennet has been inoculated, it is broken down into walnut-sized lumps. At this point, it is transferred into hexagonal or cylindrical moulds. These are then ripened by being placed in a room kept at a temperature of 37-45°C for two or three hours. Next, they are salted in a brine bath and left to mature. When ready for the table, Ircano has a slightly acidic taste.

Rennet: liquid, calf's
Outer rind: white and thin
Body: uncooked, soft and white
Top and bottom: flat
Height/weight: 7-8 cm / 1.5 kg
Territory of origin: the municipalities of Guspini, Tertenia and San Nicolò Gerrei

Pecorino Romano DOP

Pecorino Romano is made from October to July using a mixture of fresh ewe's milk from the morning and evening milkings. Milk drawn straight from the sheep is filtered and heat-treated, poured into a cheese vat and inoculated with a starter culture of leftover whey. It is then heated to a temperature of 39°C and coagulated by the addition of lamb's rennet in paste. After 25-30 minutes, the soft curd is broken into rice-sized granules and re-cooked by heating it to a temperature of 45-48°C. Next, the curd is put in draining vats and, when all the whey has run off, is cut into lumps, transferred into moulds and pressed. This pressed curd is stamped with the DOP mark and then dry-salted several times in purpose-built rooms called *caciare* by master salters, who are much respected professionals. After salting, the cheeses are ready for ageing. Pecorino cheeses destined for the table are aged for five months while those for grating are aged for at least eight months. During the maturing process, the rounds are washed with a brine solution and sometimes wrapped in a protective film. Pecorino for export is carefully selected and encased in a dark plastic material that recalls the old custom of massaging the cheeses with oil and grease or ashes as they aged.

Rennet: paste, lamb's

Outer rind: smooth, straw-yellow in colour with green highlights. Pecorino for export – the finest quality – is wrapped in a dark plastic film to recall the ancient custom of massaging the cheeses with oil and grease or ashes as they matured

Body: firm-textured and white or straw-white in colour. May have a few eyes. Fairly elastic at the beginning of the ageing process, becoming firmer and drier with time

Top and bottom: flat, 25-30 cm in diameter

Height/weight: 20 cm / 20-35 kg

Territory of origin: the Agro Romano countryside, the province of Grosseto and the entire region of Sardinia

DOP status awarded on 1 July 1996, regulation no. 1107

Pecorino Romano acquires a rock-like appearance and consistency if sufficiently mature.

These Pecorino cheeses are not covered by the classic black wrapping that used to distinguish rounds destined for the export trade. Today, the coating has a purely decorative function.

Pecorino Sardo DOP

Pecorino Sardo is eaten both fresh and mature as a table cheese while the mature version can also be used for grating. The DOP regulations call for whole ewe's milk, which may be inoculated with a natural starter culture, and is coagulated with the addition of calf's rennet. When the curd has reached the re-quired consistency, it is broken down into walnut-sized nuggets, for the fresh version, or into sweetcorn-sized granules, if it is destined to become mature Pecorino. Next, the curd is poured into cylindrical moulds to make cylindrical cheeses with a flat top and bottom. The rounds are salted, sometimes dry but more often in a brine bath. They are then allowed to age for a period of 20 to 60 days, for fresh Pecorino, and 2 to 12 months for the mature version, which may also be smoked. Fresh Pecorino Sar-do has a smooth, thin outer rind that is white or pale straw-white in colour. Inside, it is soft, white and firm-textured with sparsely distributed eyes and has a mild, aromatic, slightly acidic flavour. The minimum fat in dry matter permissible is 40%. Mature Pecorino Sardo has a thicker, straw-yellow rind that shades into brown as it matures. The body is firm, white or straw-white, and presents a few scattered eyes. Soft and elastic in texture when young, Pecorino Sardo becomes harder, and on oc-casion grainy, as it ages. The flavour is pleasantly tangy and the minimum fat in dry matter is 35%.

Rennet: liquid, calf's (large-scale, industrial dairies). Paste, kid's or lamb's (small-scale cheesemakers)
Outer rind: fine, straw-yellow, darker in more mature cheeses
Body: elastic, semi-cooked
Top and bottom: flat, 15-20 cm in diameter
Height/weight: 6-13 cm / 1.7-4 kg
Territory of origin: the entire region
DOP status awarded on 1 July 1996, regulation no. 1107

More than seven million sheep roam the pastures of Sardinia and most of the milk they yield goes to make Pecorino Sardo cheese.

Peretta

After the milk has first been heated then cooled to a temperature of 37°C, it is inoculated with a whey-based starter culture and then rennet, although not all makers use the starter. When it has coagulated and set, the soft curd is broken down into hazelnut-sized lumps. To obtain Peretta's characteristic elastic texture, the curd is allowed to ripen for about 24 hours, after which time it becomes plastic and pliable. Next, it is stretched and modelled into the shape of a pear with a small head. The now firm curd "pears" are immersed in cold water for a short time to harden, and are then salted in a brine bath. The next stage is to hang them to age for up to 15 days. Peretta is generally eaten fresh but may also be used as an ingredient in the preparation of stuffing for ravioli, or to make *sebada*, a traditional Sardinian cake.

Rennet: liquid or powder, calf's
Outer rind: thin and smooth. Straw-white in colour
Body: straw-white in colour, firm-textured and soft
Top and bottom: curved
Height/weight: variable / 0.5-1 kg
Territory of origin: the entire region

Ricotta Gentile

To produce this type of ricotta, the whey is poured into a double-bottomed cheese vat and heated to a temperature of 80°C. As it is heated, the whey is stirred constantly until the protein starts to rise to the surface. When the proteins have solidified, they carefully transferred with a strainer into moulds in the form of truncated cones. The Ricotta is left for a short time in a cool (5-10°C) room before being packed for sale. Ricotta Gentile is also known as Ricotta Romana because its basic ingredient is the leftover whey from the production of Pecorino Romano. White in colour when ready for consumption, it has a soft creamy texture and a mild flavour. Ricotta Gentile may be eaten fresh or used as an ingredient for ravioli stuffing, cakes or other sweets.

Body: buttery, creamy white in colour
Top and bottom: smooth. The top is 10 cm in diameter and the bottom has a diameter of 20 cm
Height/weight: 8-10 cm / 1.5-2 kg
Territory of origin: the provinces of Nuoro, Cagliari, Sassari, and Oristano

Ricotta Mustia

The whey is heated to a temperature of 82-85°C and stirred constantly. When the *ricotta*, that is the proteins in the whey, are beginning to rise to the surface, stirring stops and the proteins are left to stand and solidify for 5-10 minutes. After coagulating, the Ricotta is transferred into cylindrical moulds. It is then drained by pressing it with a wooden disc overnight. Next, the cylinders are dry-salted and, 24 hours later, they are transferred for five or six hours to the smoking room, where a fire of aromatic herbs is burning. The table-ready product is cylindrical in shape, and has an amber colouring, a soft, firm texture and a slightly piquant taste.

Outer rind: fine, medium-firm in texture and amber yellow in colour
Body: soft, pressed, brownish-white in colour
Top and bottom: flat, 16-18 cm in diameter
Height/weight: 2 cm / 0.8-2 kg
Territory of origin: the entire region, particularly the province of Sassari

Semicotto Caprino

The milk is heated to a temperature of 38°C and inoculated with a small amount of whey starter, followed by calf's rennet. When the mixture has coagulated to the required consistency, the soft curd is first broken and then semi-cooked for a few minutes. Next, it is cut, put into moulds, and left to drain in a warm room for several hours. The following day, the rounds are salted by steeping them in a brine bath for about 48 hours. The product is now ready for maturing in a temperature and humidity-controlled cellar. The body of Semicotto Caprino is white and firm. If aged, the cheese has a strong flavour but the palate is more delicate in the fresh version. Semicotto Caprino is produced throughout Sardinia, and is sometimes made with goat's milk.

Rennet: liquid, kid's
Outer rind: hard and smooth. Dark brown in colour
Body: hard and semi-cooked. White in colour
Top and bottom: flat, 20-25 cm in diameter
Height/weight: 10-15 cm / 3-4 kg
Territory of origin: the provinces of Nuoro and Cagliari

Sicily

Sicily is still home to many native breeds of milk ewes, all with strong ties to their territory. The best quality Ragusano is made from the milk of Modicana sheep while only Belice ewes produce the basic ingredient of the legendary Vastedda cheese.

Caciocavallo Palermitano

Milk from a single milking is coagulated in a wooden barrel with kid's rennet. The resulting curd is broken into small pieces, wrapped in a cloth, and pressed in whey. After it has ripened in the whey, the curd is left to dry out overnight and the next day it is cut and stretched. The firm curd is moulded into shape in two stages. First, it is hand-moulded into an egg shape (*primintiu*) and then it is worked into its characteristic quadrilateral using a traditional wooden tool (*rotula*). The cheeses are then left to age in cool, well-ventilated rooms, where they remain for one to three months. Caciocavallo is used as an ingredient in dishes such as *sarde a beccafico* (stuffed sardines) and *timballo di maccheroni* (macaroni flan). It is an excellent complement for Sicily's red wines, such as Baglio, Eredità, Nubetonda and others. Caciocavallo from Cinisi and Godrano, made from the milk of Cinisara cows raised wild in open pastures, is particularly highly prized.

Rennet: paste, kid's
Outer rind: solid, lustrous, straw-yellow or yellow-brown in colour
Body: plastic, cooked and semi-hard. Straw-yellow in colour, shading into gold
Top and bottom: flat, rectangular, 30-45 cm in length
Height/weight: 12-18 cm / 3-10 kg
Territory of origin: the provinces of Palermo and Trapani, in particular the areas of Godrano and Cinisi

Canestrato

The milk is heated to a temperature of 37°C, poured into a wooden barrel, and inoculated with a paste of lamb's rennet. The soft curd is strained off and put into moulds – in this case, rush baskets – that give the final cheese its characteristic shape. As it is put in the moulds, the curd is pressed by hand and black peppercorns or flakes of chilli pepper may be added. It is then cooked at a temperature of 80°C and left to dry on large wooden boards. The following day, the rounds are dry-salted with sea salt until they can absorb no more, and a layer of salt forms on the surface. Next, they are left to mature in very cool, well-ventilated rooms, such as cellars or natural caves, and remain there for a period that varies according to the degree of maturity desired.

Rennet: paste, lamb's or kid's
Outer rind: wrinkled and lined by the rush baskets. Ochre in colour
Body: solid, varying in hardness, sometimes with very small eyes. Straw-yellow in colour
Top and bottom: flat or slightly concave, 18-35 cm in diameter
Height/weight: 12-28 cm / 5-20 kg
Territory of origin: the entire region of Sicily

Maiorchino

The milk is heated to a temperature of 39°C and coagulated with kid's or lamb's rennet in 60 minutes. The soft curd is broken into small pieces and cooked at a temperature of about 60°C. It is allowed to stand for a short time, worked back into a lump, put into moulds and pressed by hand. Holes are then punched in the curd with a fine iron rod called a *minacino*, which helps the whey to drain off. The firm curd is dry-salted for between 20 and 30 days and then oiled. Maiorchino is used for cooking, and in particular for grating over pasta dishes. The cheese also has a starring role in an old custom. In the village of Novara di Sicilia, a race is held just before Carnival in which rounds of Maiorchino are rolled down the town's main street. The round that reaches the bottom of the road first without breaking wins.

Rennet: paste, kid's or lamb's
Outer rind: hard, solid, brick-brown in colour
Body: fatty, cooked, straw-yellow in colour
Top and bottom: flat, 30-33 cm in diameter
Height/weight: 10-12 cm / 10-12 kg
Territory of origin: the mountain area of Peloritani, in particular the municipalities of Bosico, Novara di Sicilia, Montalbano di Elicona, Fondachelli, Tripi, Santa Lucia del Mela, and Mezzarrà Sant'Andrea

Pecorino Siciliano DOP

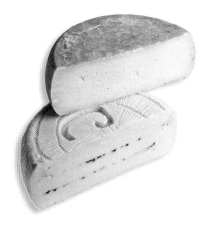

Pecorino Siciliano can boast an ancient tradition, which is documented as far back as the ancient Greeks. Pliny, too, the first writer to classify Italian and non-Italian cheeses, called it one of the best of his time. Pecorino Siciliano is made from whole raw ewe's milk. Usually, the milk from the evening milking is stored in a cool place and mixed with milk from the following morning's milking. Some sheep farms, however, make Pecorino twice a day. The milk is heated to a temperature of 37°C and a paste of lamb's rennet made using traditional techniques is inoculated, in a proportion of 100 g of rennet per 100 kg of milk. After 25-30 minutes, the soft curd is broken with a *rotula* ("curd knife") into lentil-sized particles and put in a vat of hot (75°C) water. It is skimmed off with rush baskets called *fascedde*, pressed by hand and cooked in whey at a temperature of 85°C for about three hours. The baskets are then placed on sloping boards for 24 hours to allow the remaining whey to drain off. The next stage is dry-salting, after which the cheeses are ready for the table, as "Pecorino Primo Sale". Otherwise, maturing begins, involving a second salting after 10 days, and sometimes even a third after two months. The cheeses are aged for a minimum of four months. Pecorino Siciliano is used for cooking and is a crucial ingredient in various traditional Sicilian first course dishes, such as *gnocchetti* (small potato dumplings), *maccheroni al sugo* (macaroni with meat sauce) and *bucatini alla contadina* ("country-style" pasta).

Rennet: paste, lamb's
Outer rind: ivory-white in colour, wrinkled, lined by the rush baskets in which the curd is left to drain
Body: uncooked, elastic at the beginning of the maturing process, later becoming harder and more solid. Ivory-white in colour, with reddish streaks, often studded with whole black peppercorns
Top and bottom: flat or slightly concave, 18-35 cm in diameter
Height/weight: 12-28 cm / 4-12 kg
Territory of origin: the entire region of Sicily
DOP status awarded on 12 June 1996, regulation no. 1107

Pecorino Siciliano can be eaten fresh from the dairy (known as "Tuma"), after two weeks' ageing ("Primo Sale") and after 50 days' maturing (semi-mature). Only cheeses that have been matured for at least four months, with or without peppercorns, can bear the DOP mark.

Piacentino

The milk is heated in a container known as a *quadara* and co-agulated with kid's or lamb's rennet, usually produced on the premises. The soft curd is broken up vigorously with a *ruotula* ("curd knife") into rice-sized granules and then 10% hot water is added. The *lacciata* ("curd") is allowed to settle on the bottom of the pan and stand for about a quarter of an hour. It is then strained off, put into rush containers, and cooked rapidly in hot whey. After two or three days, the cheese moves on to be dry-salted for about one month and is then matured. Piacentino can be eaten fresh as a table cheese, or may be used for grating.

Rennet: paste, kid's or lamb's
Outer rind: hard, wrinkled, brown in colour
Body: uncooked, soft, straw-yellow in colour shading into gold or saffron
Top and bottom: slightly concave, 18-30 cm in diameter
Height/weight: 22-35 cm / 6-14 kg
Territory of origin: the municipalities in the hinterland of the province of Enna

Provola dei Nebrodi

P rovola dei Nebrodi is a traditional Sicilian cheese made by small-scale cheesemakers who pass down their craft techniques from one generation to the next. The milk is heated to a temperature of 45°C and inoculated with lamb's or kid's rennet. Once it has coagulated, the soft curd is broken up into peanut-sized lumps, hot water is added and it is left to ripen for about 12 hours. The next stage is to stretch the curd in hot water and mould it. The cheeses are then salted in brine and allowed to mature for several days before being left to age in cool, well-ventilated rooms. Their taste varies from mild to tangy as ageing progresses. Provola dei Nebrodi is an excellent table cheese but is also used as an ingredient in various traditional Sicilian dishes.

Rennet: paste, lamb's or kid's
Outer rind: smooth and lustrous. Amber-tinged straw-yellow in colour
Body: plastic, uncooked, straw-white in colour
Top and bottom: smooth, 10-20 cm in diameter
Height/weight: 20-30 cm / 1-1.5 kg
Territory of origin: the territory of the municipalities of Capizzi in the province of Messina, of Cerami and Nicosia in the province of Enna, and the neighbouring areas

Provola delle Madonie

The milk is heated to a temperature of 37-38°C and inoculated, in traditional wooden barrels or in a copper cauldron, with a paste of lamb's rennet. When the curd has attained the desired consistency, it is cut into hazelnut-sized lumps. It then sours in hot water or hot whey for a certain time and is strained off and left to dry on a large wooden board. Once dry, the firm curd is cut into thin slices that are put back into the wooden barrel and soaked in water heated to a temperature of 85°C. The curd is then stretched with the aid of a stick and, when it is judged to be elastic enough, it is modelled into small pear shapes. The cheeses are tied together in pairs and hung over a pole in a cool, well-ventilated room, where they mature for 10-15 days.

Rennet: paste, lamb's
Outer rind: smooth and thin. Straw-yellow in colour
Body: firm, supple and elastic. Ivory-white to straw-yellow in colour
Top and bottom: smooth and curved
Height/weight: 10-30 cm / 1-1.2 kg
Territory of origin: the entire Monti delle Madonie area

COW'S MILK

Ragusano DOP

This cheese has been an integral part of Sicily's history and culture for hundreds of years. In the sixteenth century, cheeses from Ragusa were being exported and traded as far away as Zara in Dalmatia. Ragusano is essentially a Caciocavallo with a very unusual shape known as *scaluni*, which means "step" in the Sicilian dialect. The shape was probably found to be particularly practical in the years after the First World War, when Ragusano was in great demand from Sicilian emigrants to the United States. They persuaded producers to increase the size of the cheeses, which up until then had weighed seven to eight kilos each. Ragusano is made with whole raw milk from cows, usually of the Modicana breed, that have been raised practically wild in the aromatic herb-rich pastures of the Monti Iblei area. The milk is heated to a temperature of 34°C and coagulated with kid's or lamb's rennet in 60-90 minutes. Next, the soft curd is broken into small pieces in two stages, hot water being added to the curd in the pan in between. When it is ready, the curd is strained off, left to ripen, then stretched and shaped into its characteristic form. The cheese is salted in brine and left to mature for a varying period of time. After as little as one week, fresh Ragusano is ready for the table but it can be aged for up to four months. Matured Ragusano has a mouth-filling, tangy flavour. Ragusano may be served in slices or slivers with vegetables and can also be used for grating. It is also be cut into thick slices, coated in breadcrumbs and fried. Ragusano's territory of origin has been identified as the municipalities of Acote, Chiaramonte Gulfi, Comiso, Giarratana, Ispica, Modica, Monterosso Almo, Ragusa, Santa Croce Camerina, Sciali and Vittoria in the province of Ragusa, and the municipalities of Noto, Palazzolo Acreide and Rosolini in the province of Siracusa.

Rennet: paste, kid's or lamb's
Outer rind: firm, thin, varying in colour from blond to straw-yellow
Body: cooked, plastic, elastic or hard. Straw-yellow or golden yellow in colour
Top and bottom: flat, rectangular
Height/weight: 10-15 cm / 12-16 kg
Territory of origin: parts of the provinces of Ragusa and Siracusa
DOP status awarded on 11 July 1996, regulation no. 1263

The finest Ragusano is made from the milk of Modicana cows, a native Sicilian breed that is highly adaptable and perfectly at home in Ragusa's poor quality but aromatic herb-rich pastures.

Ricotta Infornata

Sea salt or *agra* ("acid whey") is added to whey from the milk of cows, ewes or goats, or a mixture of the three, and the solution is heated to a temperature of 90°C. When the Ricotta has risen to the surface and the froth has been removed, it is poured into rush baskets, which are then placed on a sloping board. The Ricotta is left to drain for one or two days and then transferred into a greased pottery container. The cheese is now sprinkled with ground black pepper and then baked in a stone oven at 180-200°C for about 30 minutes. When a delicate reddish-brown skin has formed, the Ricotta Infornata is taken out of the oven and put on a plate to stand for 24 hours.

Outer rind: thin, reddish-brown in colour
Body: creamy, ivory-white in colour
Top and bottom: smooth, 10-12 cm in diameter
Height/weight: 2 cm / variable
Territory of origin: the entire region of Sicily

Vastedda della Valle del Belice

The milk is heated to a temperature of 36°C and inoculated with lamb's rennet. Coagulation takes about half an hour. The soft curd is first broken down into rice-sized granules. It is then worked into a lump and put into baskets, which used to be woven from rushes but are now made of plastic, before being left to drain. The following day, the now firm curd is cut into slices and stretched in leftover whey from Ricotta production. Finally, it is put into soup plates, called *vastedde* in the local dialect, to be moulded and then immersed in brine for salting. The cheese is ready for the table in about 48 hours. Vastedda is used in the kitchen to make a variety of dishes, including *insalata campagnola* (country salad), *timballo di maccheroni* (macaroni flan) and the origano-based *riamata del Belice*. This is one of the few stretched-curd Italian cheeses made exclusively from whole ewe's milk.

Rennet: paste, lamb's
Outer rind: fine-skinned, straw-white in colour
Body: plastic, soft and lustrous. White or straw-white in colour
Top and bottom: flat, 8-10 cm in diameter
Height/weight: 2 cm / up to 3 kg
Territory of origin: the municipalities of Gibellina, Poggioreale, Salaparuta, Salemi, Santa Ninfa, Vita, Castelvetrano, Campobello di Mazara and Calatafini in the province of Trapani, Santa Margherita Belice, Montevago, Menfi and Sambuca in the province of Agrigento, Contessa Entellina in the province of Palermo, and all the municipalities in Valle del Belice

Tuscany

Tuscany is synonymous with Pecorino, the cheese that best embodies the character of the territory. There is significant production of various kinds of Pecorino all over the region, from the Garfagnana to the Maremma, from Val d'Orcia to Chianti, and from the Casentino to the Apennines.

Caciotta Toscana

Caciotta is one of the most popular cheeses in Tuscany. Generally, it is made with pasteurised milk for immediate consumption. When the milk has been heated to about 40°C, calf's rennet is added and about 20 minutes later, the soft curd is broken up into walnut-sized lumps. It is then placed in moulds and the whey is drained off. To encourage draining, the rounds are heated to 45-50°C for about an hour. Salting is carried out in a brine bath, where the rounds remain for 8-16 hours. Caciotta is ready for the table after maturing for about 20 days at a temperature ranging from 8-19°C, in rooms with humidity as high as 60%. The rounds are turned over and washed frequently during maturing.

Rennet: liquid, calf's
Outer rind: slightly dimpled, in various shades of yellow
Body: fatty, firm and straw-yellow in colour
Top and bottom: flat, 14-20 cm in diameter
Height/weight: 5-8 cm / 0.8 –1.5 kg
Territory of origin: the whole of Tuscany and Maremma in particular

Marzolino del Chianti

Warm, raw milk from the morning milking is used mixed with milk drawn the previous evening. It is heated to 30-32°C and inoculated with vegetable rennet. After a period of one to three hours, the soft curd is ready to be broken up into granules the size of a grain of sweetcorn. It is then removed from the whey, pressed and shaped into ovals. Next, the curd is transferred into concave moulds to drain off the whey. Draining is completed by pressing the rounds. The pressed curd is dry-salted and then inserted into a *saccola*, or cloth bag, and hung for about two days, during which time the rounds are turned over every eight hours or so. Marzolino ripens for a further seven days in the cellar, where the rounds are again regularly turned over and washed. Finally, the cheese goes on to maturing, which can last for up to six months. During maturing, the forms are brushed with oil or oil dregs.

Rennet: vegetable rennet from the flower of the cardoon (*Cynara cardunculus silvestris*), in powder or as an infusion
Outer rind: with a light or heavy "orange-peel" effect, depending on maturing. Yellow to reddish in colour
Body: white, tending to straw-white in colour
Top and bottom: curved
Height/weight: 9-13 cm / 0.5 –1.5 kg
Territory of origin: the area between Florence and Siena, crossed by the steep valleys of the Greve, Pesa and Arbia

Pecorino Baccellone

The milk, usually pasteurised, is heated to about 36°C, salted and inoculated with calf's rennet. About half an hour later, the soft curd can be broken into walnut-sized lumps. The whey is then removed and the curd transferred to special moulds to drain. Further draining may be encouraged by placing the moulds for two hours in a room warmed to 30°C and lightly pressing them. Next, the rounds are salted in a brine bath for 24 hours. After salting, they are ripened for two to five days in a cool (8°C), damp (90% humidity) environment. They are regularly turned over and washed during this period. At this point, the Pecorino Baccellone is ready for the table.

Rennet: liquid, calf's
Body: white, creamy
Top and bottom: flat, 15-20 cm in diameter
Height/weight: 7-15 cm / 1-3 kg
Territory of origin: the entire region of Tuscany

Pecorino della Garfagnana

The milk used for this Pecorino comes from Massese cattle that are raised in the wild. It is heated to 38°C and allowed to coagulate for about 20 minutes after inoculation with calf's rennet. The soft curd is then broken up into very small pieces, about the size of a grain of rice, and transferred to moulds after the whey has been drained off. Draining is completed in the moulds, although the curd may also be pressed or, very occasionally, heated in a warm room or wooden boxes. Once the firm curd is perfectly dry, the rounds are dry-salted and then left to mature for about 30 days in a cool, well-ventilated room, where they are regularly turned over and washed. Pecorino della Garfagnana is usually sold fresh, since output is very limited, but in rare cases, the cheeses are matured for about three months.

Rennet: liquid, calf's or kid's
Outer rind: firm, smooth, of varying hardness, and ranging in colour from golden yellow to brown
Body: firm, with more or less marked eyes. Pale to deep straw-white in colour.
Top and bottom: flat, 18-22 cm in diameter
Height/weight: 7-12 cm / 1.8 -3 kg
Territory of origin: the entire Garfagnana area in the province of Lucca

Pecorino di Montagna

The milk, which today is invariably pasteurised and therefore needs a starter culture, is heated to 32-34°C and inoculated with calf's rennet. The soft curd is broken down into small lumps, walnut-sized for cheese to be eaten fresh and rice-sized for the mature version. It is then separated from the whey and transferred to moulds to drain. The draining process is encouraged by placing the moulds in a warm room (maximum 35°C) for two to six hours and pressing them lightly. Salting is carried out by immersion in a brine bath for 12-24 hours. Pecorino di Montagna then matures for 20-40 days in a cool (8°C), damp (90% humidity) room.

Rennet: liquid, calf's
Outer rind: with a light or heavy "orange-peel" effect, depending on maturing. Ash or oil dregs may be used for ageing, which gives the rind a dark brown or blackish colour
Body: soft, floury and white
Top and bottom: flat, 18-20 cm in diameter
Height/weight: 8-10 cm / 1.2 –2.5 kg
Territory of origin: the upper hill slopes and mountains of southern and central Tuscany (Amiata, Pratomagno, Colline Metallifere and Mugello)

Pecorino di Pienza

Regrettably, Pecorino di Pienza is another traditional cheese that is now almost always made with pasteurised milk. The milk is heated to between 30 and 40°C and inoculated with calf's rennet. After about half an hour, the soft curd is broken up into hazelnut-sized lumps and transferred into moulds. Further draining of the whey is encouraged by placing the rounds in a room heated to about 35°C for two hours. Next comes salting, which may be either dry or in a brine bath. Pecorino di Pienza requires a ripening period of 20 days, during which time the rounds are regularly turned over and washed. Ripening takes place in a cool (10-14°C), damp (80% humidity) room. Finally, there comes maturing, which may last anything from 40 days to two months. During maturing, the cheeses are treated with oil and tomato.

Rennet: liquid, calf's
Outer rind: with a light or heavy "orange-peel" effect, depending on maturing. Deep yellow in colour, with pink shading acquired from treatment with oil ad tomato during maturing
Body: firm and elastic. White, tending to straw-white in colour
Top and bottom: flat, 14-20 cm in diameter
Height/weight: 4-8 cm / 0.8 –1.8 kg
Territory of origin: the southern part of the province of Siena, including the municipalities of Pienza, Montepulciano, San Quirico d'Orcia, Radicofani, Castiglion d'Orcia, Torrita di Siena, Trequanda, San Giovanni d'Asso and Montalcino

Pecorino Senese

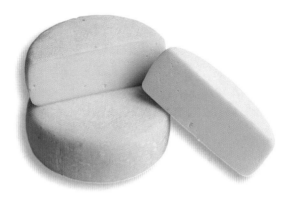

The milk is heated to 36-37°C and inoculated with calf's rennet. After 20-30 minutes, the soft curd is broken up into hazelnut-sized lumps, separated from the whey, and then placed in moulds to drain. Further draining is carried out by placing the curd in wooden boxes for half an hour, in the case of fresh Pecorino, and for about two hours for the mature version. Salting is normally done in a brine bath for about 12 hours but dry-salting is sometimes preferred. After ripening for 20 days at a humidity of 80-90% and a temperature of 8-10°C, the fresh cheese is ready to go on sale. Otherwise, it is matured for a moderate length of time, during which it is treated with olive oil, oil dregs and tomato, and regularly turned over.

Rennet: liquid, calf's
Outer rind: yellow, with highlights in various other shades
Body: firm, soft, buttery and white, tending to straw-yellow in colour
Top and bottom: flat, 12-18 cm in diameter
Height/weight: 5-8 cm / 0.8 –1.2 kg
Territory of origin: Siena, neighbouring municipalities and the Sienese part of the Valdelsa

Pecorino Toscano DOP

The name "Pecorino" is a recent invention. Until the end of the Second World War, every area in Tuscany had its own "Cacio" with a different name, even though the cheesemaking techniques used were very similar. Today, ewe's milk, produced in the area defined by the DOP regulations, is usually pasteurised to make Pecorino, although there is a movement among small-scale cheesemakers to revert to using raw milk. It is coagulated by inoculation with calf's rennet at a temperature of 35-38°C, which takes about 25 minutes. If soft Pecorino is required, the curd is then broken up into hazelnut-sized lumps. For cheese destined for longer maturing, which will have a semi-hard texture, the curd is broken into smaller pieces and may also be reheated to 40-44°C. The curd is then transferred to cheese hoops to allow the whey to drain. This is encouraged by pressing the rounds manually or by steam-treatment – a procedure that causes a rapid drop in the cheese's pH – for 30 minutes to three and a half hours. Salting is carried out by immersing the cheese in a brine bath for at least eight hours, in the case of soft Pecorino, and 12-14 hours for the hard version. Dry-salting is also sometimes employed. The soft version matures for at least 20 days while semi-hard Pecorino remains in the cellar for at least four months at 8-10°C with a humidity of 80-90%. Fat in dry matter is never less that 45% in the fresh cheese and 40% in the mature version. Pecorino Toscano

DOP is made all over the region as well as in a few municipalities in Umbria (Allerona and Castiglion del Lago) and Lazio (Acquapendente, Onano, San Lorenzo Nuovo, Grotte di Castro, Gradoli, Valentano, Farnese, Ischia di Castro, Montefiascone, Bolsena and Capodimonte).

Rennet: liquid, calf's
Outer rind: yellow
Body: firm and supple
Top and bottom: flat, 15-22 cm in diameter
Height/weight: 7-11 cm / 1-3 kg
Territory of origin: the entire region of Tuscany as well as some municipalities in Umbria and Lazio
DOP status awarded on 1 July 1996, regulation no. 1263

The designation Pecorino Toscano embraces the whole of the region's production of this type of cheese. However, it includes many distinct varieties that differ in the characteristics of the grazing territory, the breed of sheep involved, and the cheesemaking technique used.

Raviggiolo di Pecora

Pasteurised milk is heated to 36-37°C, salted and inoculated with calf's rennet. After about one hour, the soft curd is cut into large lumps, which are carefully removed from the whey without breaking them. They are then placed in moulds to drain. The process may be encouraged by placing the moulds in a warm room for an hour. Raviggiolo ripens for two days at 5°C in a room with 100% humidity, after which it is ready for the table.

Rennet: liquid, calf's
Body: white, with straw-white highlights
Top and bottom: flat, 12-20 cm in diameter
Height/weight: 3-6 cm / 0.5-1.2 kg
Territory of origin: the entire region

Trentino Alto Adige

The Alpine pastures of this largely mountainous region have long yielded characterful cheeses of impeccable breeding. Two of the most outstanding are the hard-to-find Vezzena and the pungently aromatic Puzzone di Moena.

Almkäse

Most Almkäse, one of the region's oldest cheeses, is made in mountain dairies. Its name derives from *Alm*, the German word for "Alpine pasture". Part-skimmed raw milk is heated to 32°C and inoculated with powdered rennet. After it has coagulated, the soft curd is broken up into granules the size of a pea or grain of sweetcorn. It is then semi-cooked at 38-40°C, over a wood fire, if the cheese is made in the mountains. The curd is then removed, cut up into large lumps and transferred to moulds, where it is pressed for 24 hours. The following day, the pressed curd is taken out of the mould and immersed in a brine bath for 48 hours. Next, the rounds are matured in cool, damp rooms where they will remain for at least three months. During maturing, the cheeses are turned over, scraped and brushed every day.

Rennet: powder, calf's
Outer rind: smooth and firm. Deep yellow in colour, tending to brown
Body: firm and uneven, with variable, unevenly distributed eyes. Ivory-white shading into deep straw-yellow in colour
Top and bottom: flat, 35-40 cm in diameter
Height/weight: 8-10 cm / 7-14 kg
Territory of origin: all over the mountain areas of Alto Adige, and Val Venosta in particular

Bergkäse

A relatively new cheese, first produced about 20 years ago, Bergkäse nevertheless remains faithful to the cheesemaking tradition of Val Pusteria and is made only with local milk. Whole or part-skimmed milk, usually pasteurised, is inoculated with milk enzymes and heated to 32°C, when calf's rennet in powder is added. About 30 minutes later, the soft curd is broken up into pea-sized lumps and then cooked at 40°C for about 50 minutes. After cooking, the curd is removed, placed on a table, cut and transferred into moulds. The following day, the rounds are immersed in brine, where they will remain for two days. After salting, the cheeses are stored in a warm environment for three weeks, then in a cooler, damper room, where they will complete the maturing process in about ten weeks.

Rennet: powder, calf's
Outer rind: hard, firm, smooth and brownish in colour
Body: firm and solid, with irregularly distributed and often rather large eyes. Straw-yellow in colour
Top and bottom: flat, 40 cm in diameter
Height/weight: 10 cm / 10-12 kg
Territory of origin: the entire Upper Val Pusteria

Caprino di Cavalese

Caprino was once made all over Val di Fiemme but today, goat's milk produced in the valley is taken to the cheese dairy at Cavalese, which now is only maker of this traditional product. The milk is heated to 31°C and inoculated with rennet. The soft curd is then broken into small pieces and cooked at 44°C until the desired consistency is obtained. Next, the curd is transferred into moulds and dry-salted. The rounds are treated until they no longer absorb salt. After this, the cheeses go on to maturing, which was once carried out in the earth or stone-floored cellars of the mountain farms, but today is done in cool, damp, purpose-built rooms. While maturing, the cheeses are turned over and moistened with a brine solution once a week.

Rennet: paste, calf's or lamb's
Outer rind: thin, tending to reddish-yellow with maturing
Body: firm, with a sparse or plentiful eyes, and ivory-white in colour
Top and bottom: flat, 15-25 cm in diameter
Height/weight: 8-10 cm / 3-4 kg
Territory of origin: the municipalities of Cavalese and Fiavé Pinzolo

Graukäse

This is a cheese with a long tradition in the Tyrol. It takes its name from the greyish (*grau*) colour of its body. Graukäse is obtained by acid coagulation only. Nothing is actually added to the milk. The cream is allowed to rise to the top and the milk is then part-skimmed before being heated to 25°C and left to coagulate naturally, a process which may take as long as 36 hours. The soft curd is then stirred slowly and the mixture is lightly cooked at 40°C. The curd is removed and pressed for about half an hour. It is then crumbled, seasoned with salt and pepper and placed in moulds, where it stands at a temperature of 20°C for 24 hours. Subsequently, the cheese is matured for a week in a cellar with very high humidity.

Body: grainy, tender and uneven, tending to grey in colour
Top and bottom: irregular
Height/weight: varying from 1-1.5 kg
Territory of origin: the entire eastern part of alto Adige, especially Valle Aurina

Lagundo or Bauernkäse

Part-skimmed milk is pasteurised, then cooled to 32°C and inoculated with a starter culture and powdered calf's rennet. When it has coagulated, which takes an average of 35 minutes, the curd is broken up into cherry-sized lumps and then semi-cooked at 42°C for 20 minutes. The curd is left to stand for 15 minutes and then transferred to the moulds, where it will remain for eight hours. When it is taken out of the moulds, the firm curd goes into a brine bath for about two days. Subsequently, the cheeses are placed for eight weeks in a cool (13°C), damp (98% humidity) room, where they are turned over and washed every week.

Rennet: powder, calf's
Outer rind: hard, smooth and dark brown in colour
Body: springy, with close-packed, evenly distributed eyes. Straw-white in colour
Top and bottom: flat, 35 cm in diameter
Height/weight: 10 cm / 7 kg
Territory of origin: the mountain dairies of Velloi, Rio Lagundo, Rablà, Parcines, Tablà and Monte Sole

Nostrano Fiavé

This "Nostrano" ("local") belongs to the *de casèl* family, Trentino's most traditional group of cheeses. Nevertheless, Fiavé's eyes and flavour are distinctly reminiscent of Asiago. The cheese is made by heating part-skimmed milk to 32-35°C and inoculating it with powdered rennet. Thirty minutes later, the curd is broken up in two stages until it is in sweetcorn-sized lumps. After cutting, it is cooked briefly at 44-46°C. Next, the curd is gathered up in cloths and transferred to moulds, where it stands for six to eight hours. The rounds are turned over in this period. The next stage is salting in a brine bath for three to five days, or dry-salting for eight days. The cheeses are then transferred to a very damp (90% humidity) room where they mature at 12-16°C for about four months, during which time the rounds are regularly turned over and washed with brine, or in some cases with whey.

Rennet: powder, calf's
Outer rind: firm, thin, deep yellow or brownish in colour
Body: elastic, with plentiful eyes of varying sizes. Pale to deep straw-white in colour.
Top and bottom: flat, with a slightly raised edge, 30-35 cm in diameter
Height/weight: 10-11 cm / 7-9 kg
Territory of origin: all of the area around the Massiccio del Lagorai

Nostrano Val di Fassa

The best Nostrano cheeses are the ones made in mountain dairies during the summer months. The cheesemaking technique Nostrano Val di Fassa is similar to that used for Puzzone. Part-skimmed raw milk is heated to 36°C and inoculated with powdered rennet. After coagulation, which may take 25-30 minutes, the curd is cut into sweetcorn-sized granules and then semi-cooked at a temperature of 43-45°C for 20 minutes. After transfer into moulds, the curd is pressed and salted in a brine bath after being left to stand for a while. Next comes maturing, the most crucial stage in cheesemaking and the procedure that will determine the product's final taste profile. For this, the rounds are placed in a very damp room, where they will be washed with a tepid salt solution several times a week. Nostrano takes 40 days to mature but ageing is usually extended for as long as five or six months. The resulting product is an ideal complement for polenta-based dishes of the Trentino kitchen.

Rennet: powder, calf's
Outer rind: smooth, damp, with an oily sheen. Brick red in colour
Body: firm, elastic, with a few eyes, and white or straw-white in colour
Top and bottom: flat, 35 cm in diameter
Height/weight: 8-10 cm / 9-10 kg
Territory of origin: Val di Fassa and Conca del Primiero

Puzzone di Moena

Raw milk from two milkings, one part-skimmed, is heated to 36°C and inoculated with powdered rennet. About 25 minutes later, the curd is broken up into sweetcorn-sized lumps and then semi-cooked at 43-46°C for about 20 minutes. The whey is then drained off. When the curd is dry, it is removed and transferred into moulds. The rounds are pressed for five or six minutes and then turned over. The cloths are then changed and the rounds are returned to the moulds for seven hours. After a further 24 hours, the cheeses are salted in a brine bath for two and a half days. Next, the nascent Puzzone is matured in very damp rooms at a temperature of 13-14°C for at least three months. During this time, it is washed with a warm salt solution once or twice every week. It is thanks to this procedure that Puzzone acquires its distinctive taste profile. Technically, it could be described as a "washed-rind" cheese.

Rennet: powder, calf's
Outer rind: smooth, soft and damp, with an oily sheen. Reddish-brown in colour
Body: firm, with a few, evenly distributed eyes. Straw-white in colour
Top and bottom: flat, 36 cm in diameter
Height/weight: 10 cm / 9 kg
Territory of origin: the municipalities of Moena and Campitello di Fassa

Spressa

The name of this cheese derives from *Spress*, a word indicating the pressed curd. Once, this was a very low-fat cheese as the milk was skimmed several times and dairy farmers were much more interested in obtaining butter than cheese. The modern version, like many mountain Nostrano cheeses, is made from skimmed milk. The milk is heated to 35-36°C, inoculated with powdered rennet, and 25-30 minutes later the curd is cut up into hazelnut-sized lumps. The soft curd is then semi-cooked at 40°C for 30 minutes, and left to stand in the whey for a further 40 minutes. It is transferred into moulds, where it is salted in a brine bath for four days. Subsequently, the rounds are matured in a cool (8°C) room, where they are turned over and brushed every day.

Rennet: powder, calf's
Outer rind: hard, firm and fairly uneven. Brown, shading into dark brown with maturing
Body: firm, elastic, with a few eyes under the rind. Straw-white in colour
Top and bottom: flat, 35 cm in diameter
Height/weight: 8-9 cm / 6-8 kg
Territory of origin: the Giudicarie area and Val Rendena

Tosela

The name derives from the verb *tosare* ("to shear"), used to de-scribe the operation of levelling off the curd before it goes in-to the mould. The cheese is made by heating fresh-drawn milk to 37-39°C and inoculating it with powdered rennet. Coagulation takes 15-20 minutes. The next stage is to cut the curd into large slices, which are then dried. The slices are left to stand for 5-10 minutes. Subsequently, the sliced curd is placed in moulds. No set shape is used for this cheese but the moulds are usually rectangu-lar. Tosela is neither salted or matured, and should be eaten as fresh as possible. Traditionally, the cheese is sliced and fried in butter with a little salt sprinkled on top.

Rennet: powder, calf's
Body: soft, elastic and very moist. Milk-white in colour
Top and bottom: may vary but are generally flat
Height/weight: varying
Territory of origin: Valle di Primiero, the Lower Val Sugana, Val di Tesino, the plateau of Asiago, and Massiccio del Lagorai

Trentingrana

A lthough Grana produced in Trento valley belongs to the *Consorzio di Tutela del Formaggio Grana*, it can have "Trentino" stamped on the rind, in compliance with the appropriate DPR regulation dated 26 January 1987. The "Trentino" mark guarantees that the round was made in Trentino but the production method is the same as that used for Parmigiano Reggiano. The cream of the evening milking is allowed to rise and is skimmed off the following morning. The morning's milk is added and the mixture is heated to 31-33°C. After inoculation with a whey-based starter culture and powdered calf's rennet, the milk coagulates and the soft curd is cut into rice-sized granules before being cooked at 53-55°C. When the curd has become elastic and reached the desired level of acidity, it is divided in two and transferred into moulds. These are then placed in brine baths. The above operations generally take 26-28 days, after which the Grana is ready for its twelve-month stay in the maturing rooms at a temperature of 18-20°C and 85% humidity.

Rennet: powder, calf's
Outer rind: hard, even-textured, smooth and lustrous. Yellow-brown in colour
Body: crumbly and grainy, becoming rock hard after maturing and with barely perceptible eyes. Straw-yellow in colour
Top and bottom: flat, 35-40 cm in diameter
Height/weight: 8-25 cm / 35-40 kg
Territory of origin: the entire province of Trento

Vezzena

V ezzena is one of Trentino's most ancient and prestigious cheeses. The Austro-Hungarian emperor Franz Josef insisted that it should always be on his table. Indeed, it is outstanding both as a table cheese and when grated over soup or pasta. Vezzena is made by heating to 34-35°C two parts whole milk with one of milk part-skimmed by allowing the cream to rise. Powdered rennet is then added, and the mixture coagulates in 15-20 minutes. The soft curd is broken into rice-sized granules and cooked at 45°C for 10 minutes. It is then removed and placed in moulds, where it is left to stand for three or four days. Next, the rounds are dry-salted, a process that takes 12 days. After salting, the cheeses are placed in a damp (80% humidity) room at 17°C, where they will mature for 90 days. During this period, the rounds are turned over frequently, greased with coconut oil at least once a week, and regularly brushed. Maturing takes an average of at least six months.

Rennet: powder, calf's
Outer rind: thin and elastic. Straw-yellow tending to brown in colour
Body: firm, even-textured and straw-yellow in colour, becoming grainy and suitable for use as a grating cheese with ageing
Top and bottom: flat, 35-40 cm in diameter
Height/weight: 8-10 cm / 8-12 kg
Territory of origin: the plateau of Vezzena, Lavarone and Fogaria

Ziger (Zigercäse)

The name of this cheese may derive from the Celtic word *tsi-gros*, meaning "cheese", or more probably from the German *Ziege*, or "goat". Whatever the case, Ziger is a very ancient cheese that was once made over a vast area of the Alps. Today, very little is produced, although a few dairies market an industrial version. The milk is part-skimmed by allowing the fat to rise to the surface, and is then heated to 30°C and inoculated with buttermilk. Acid coagulation is complete after about 48 hours. Some cheesemakers break up the curd into walnut-sized lumps while others pour it directly into cloth bags to drain. The following day, the curd is poured out onto a table and kneaded with chives, salt and pepper. After it has been shaped by hand, the Ziger is ready either for the table or for maturing, a process that lasts six to eight weeks.

Rennet: buttermilk, a by-product of buttermaking
Outer rind: the surface has a pink sheen
Body: soft, dirty white or yellowish in colour, shading into grey
Top and bottom: varying
Height/weight: varying from 0.3-1 kg
Territory of origin: Val Pusteria and the Lower Val d'Isarco to the Belluno Dolomites

Umbria

Sadly, the "garden of Italy" does not have a cheesemaking tradition to equal its natural beauty, olive oil and wine production, or wealth of historic monuments. Pecorino, in a variety of styles, is the main product, the finest of these being the so-called "Pecorino di Montagna", or Mountain Pecorino.

Pecorino di Norcia

Pasteurised milk is inoculated with a thermophilic starter culture and heated to 40°C. Rennet is then added. After 20 minutes, the soft curd is broken up into sweetcorn-sized granules and then placed in moulds to allow the whey to drain. Further draining is encouraged by ripening the product in large chests for three hours. Salting for 48 hours is carried out in brine baths. The Pecorino matures over 30 days in rooms at 80-90% humidity, and is then aged for up to six months, during which time the cheeses are treated with olive oil.

Rennet: paste, lamb's or kid's
Outer rind: slightly or heavily wrinkled, depending on the maturing period
Body: white, tending to straw-white in colour
Top and bottom: flat, 15-25 cm in diameter
Height/weight: 8-14 cm / 3 -5 kg
Territory of origin: The Upper Val Nerina, including the municipalities of Norcia, Cascia, Preci, Monteleone di Spoleto, and Poggiodomo

Valle d'Aosta

O ne cheese, Fontina, is sufficient on its own to summarise the characteristics of the entire region's production. Fontina is the ideal expression of the territory's unique character, its history, its hard-working people and their love for the mountains they live in.

Fontina DOP

There are various explanations for this cheese's name. Some link it with the mountain pastures of Fontin, in the municipality of Quart, others to the place name, Fontinaz, and still others to the surname of a family of cheesemakers. Whatever the truth, this is Valle d'Aosta's cheese *par excellence*. Yet, despite its popularity, the mountain dairy version in particular is a difficult cheese to make successfully. Only fresh milk from Valdostana cows is used. It must be raw and come from a single milking (the cheese is in fact made twice every day). The milk is heated to no more than 36°C and inoculated with natural or industrial rennet. Coagulation takes 40-50 minutes. The next stage is to stir the soft curd and break it up roughly for the first time. After being left to stand for a short while, the curd is cut again until rice-sized granules are obtained. The curd is then semi-cooked and left to settle on the bottom of the vat. Next, it wrapped up in a cloth and placed in the moulds that give the side of the cheese its characteristic concave profile. The cheeses are then pressed for about 12 hours and turned over frequently before being transferred to a cool, humid (85%) room. Here, they are turned over daily, and salted and washed with brine-soaked brushes every other day. This operation is repeated until the outer rind acquires its characteristic brown colouring. After this, the cheeses are matured in a natural environment (including caves, grottoes, former army emplacements – the co-operative dairy even uses an old copper mine), where they will stay for at least three months.

Rennet: calf's in liquid, powder or very occasionally pellet form
Outer rind: firm, thin, dark yellow or reddish-brown in colour
Body: soft, buttery and fondant, with relatively few, "bird's-eye"-sized holes. Varying in colour from straw-white to deep yellow
Top and bottom: flat, 30-45 cm in diameter
Height/weight: 7-10 cm / 8 -18 kg
Territory of origin: the entire region
DOP status awarded on 12 June 1996, regulation no. 1107

The mark of this celebrated mountain cheese features the outline of the Matterhorn. The scattered eyes presented on cutting may be observed in the illustration.

Réblèque

The dairy-produced version of this cheese, made with the surface portion of the curd, should not be confused with traditional Réblèque, the cheesemaking process for which is relatively complex. The cream that has risen is skimmed off and heated to a temperature of 35-40°C. Next, sufficient rennet is added to coagulate the cream in one and a half hours. The soft curd is lifted out whole in a cloth and placed in a perforated container in a warm, humid room. Here, the excess whey drains off. The curd, however, remains fairly moist, ripening in the meantime. Réblèque should be consumed within two or three days of being made, and is generally sprinkled with sugar or cinnamon before serving. The former President of Italy, Einaudi, who often holidayed at By in Valpelline, used to love this cheese.

Rennet: liquid, calf's
Body: creamy, soft and still moist with whey
Height/weight: irregular
Territory of origin: produced all over the Valle d'Aosta, almost exclusively in mountain dairies

Salignon

Technically speaking, Salignon is not a cheese but a Ricotta. It comes from the German cheesemaking tradition, and in particular the Walser heritage. Fairly fatty, fresh Ricotta, obtained by adding milk or cream to the whey, is used. First, it is strained, then kneaded with salt and powdered red chilli pepper, or paprika, which gives it its characteristic deep pink colour and markedly piquant flavour. Some cheesemakers also add wild herbs or dried flowers from the mountain pastures. The aromatised product is then shaped into balls, which are placed inside the hood of the hearth to dry and absorb a little smoke. There is also an unsmoked version, to which garlic is added during kneading. Salignon is generally made for consumption in the home and is rarely found on sale. It is an excellent cheese to serve with beer.

Body: crumbly, fatty, and usually aromatised with herbs and spices
Weight: variable
Territory of origin: the Lower Valle d'Aosta

COW'S, AND GOAT'S MILK
Valle d'Aosta Fromadzo DOP

A low-fat cheese made with cow's milk from two milkings, left to stand and skimmed after the cream has risen to the top, Valle d'Aosta Fromadzo may contain up to 10% goat's milk. A medium-fat version is also made, for which the milk is left to stand for 12-24 hours, as well as an extra low-fat type, in which case the milk stands for at least 36 hours. After skimming, the milk is heated to 34-36°C and inoculated with calf's rennet. When it has coagulated, the soft curd is cut into rice-sized granules and the temperature is raised to 42-45°C. At this point, the curd is placed in cheese hoops, called *feitchie* in the local dialect, where it is pressed and turned over three or four times a day. The rounds are then dry-salted, initially every other day, and then less and less frequently. After salting, the cheeses are matured in temperature-controlled rooms at 60% humidity, where they will remain for a period ranging from three months to about one year. Valle d'Aosta Fromadzo, which can also be designated in French, has a straw-yellow outer rind that tends to shade into grey with the passage of time, also acquiring reddish highlights. The body is firm, with a few small or medium-sized eyes while the proportion of fat in dry matter is less than 20% in the low-fat version and between 20 and 35% for the medium-fat. The DOP regulations permit aromatisation with the seeds or other parts of aromatic plants.

VALLE D'AOSTA

284

Rennet: liquid, calf's

Outer rind: fairly firm, varying in colour from straw-yellow to reddish-grey with maturing

Body: firm, elastic, with faint eyes, varying in colour from milk-white to deep yellow

Top and bottom: flat, 15-30 cm in diameter

Height/weight: 5-20 cm / 1 -7 kg

Territory of origin: the entire Valle d'Aosta

DOP status awarded on 1 July 1996, regulation no. 1263

Fortunately, production of this classic Alpine cheese is on the increase after a long period of near-total absence from the market.

Veneto

Asiago and Monte Veronese, whether d'Allevo ("farm-house"), pressed or whole milk, embrace virtually the entire output of the region. In addition to these two DOP cheeses, there are also specialities such as Morlacco, Formaggio Embriago (literally, "tipsy cheese"), Schiz and Cansiglio.

Asiago d'Allevo DOP

A cheese that originates from the Asiago plateau it is named after, Altopiano d'Asiago is made in the mountain pastures or
larger dairies where it is matured – one might say *allevato* (literally, "raised") – with particular care. Raw milk from Pezzata Nera
and Bruno Alpina cows is allowed to stand for 6-12 hours and the
cream that rises is skimmed off. Milk from two milkings, only the
first of which should be skimmed, can also be used. Coagulation
takes place at 35°C in 25-30 minutes. The soft curd is then broken up finely and cooked twice, first at 40°C and then at 47°C.
After being transferred into moulds, the curd is pressed first in
special wooden hoops and then in plastic hoops to stamp the
DOP mark on the rind. Next, the rounds are salted either dry or
in brine baths before maturing, which takes place on shelving in a
temperature-controlled environment. Depending on the maturing
period, Asiago may be called *mezzano* (at least three months old)
or *vecchio* (nine months old or more). The outer rind is thin and
springy, shading into brown in colour as maturing progresses. The
body is semi-hard, even-textured and straw-white, with occasional
small or medium-sized eyes for the Mezzano version. In the Vecchio or Stravecchio versions, which may also be used for grating,
the body becomes hard and grainy. At first, the palate is mild but
it gradually becomes fuller and more fragrant as the months pass.
Asiago d'Allevo Vecchio and Stravecchio made in the province of

Trento, and especially on the plateaux of Vezzena, Lavarone and Folgaria, is also known as Vezzena. During the Middle Ages, there were many flocks producing exclusively ewe's milk cheese and to-day, the dialect term used by older mountain-dwellers to indicate Asiago is still *Pegorin*, or "sheep's cheese".

Rennet: liquid or powder, calf's
Outer rind: thin and springy, shading into brown with maturing
Body: semi-hard, even-textured and straw-white, with occasional small or medium-sized eyes for the Mezzano version, hard and grainy for the Vecchio and Stravecchio cheeses
Top and bottom: flat or almost flat, 30-36 cm in diameter
Height/weight: 9-12 cm / 8-12 kg
Territory of origin: the provinces of Vicenza and Trento, the hill country and low-lying area beneath to the west of the river Piave in the province of Treviso, and some municipalities in the province of Padua
DOP status awarded on 12 June 1996, regulation no. 1107

Asiago d'Allevo is the more suitable cheese for prolonged ageing of the two types permitted by the Asiago DOP regulations. In some cases, the body becomes rock hard, as can be seen from the photograph, and the tangy palate is correspondingly fierce.

Asiago Pressato

In contrast with Asiago d'Allevo, Asiago Pressato is made in low-lying areas, and generally in fairly large dairies. The milk employed is also different, for it is pasteurised, and the salting techniques involves dry-salting the curd as soon as it comes out of the whey, and then a brine bath after pressing. Coagulation takes place at 36°C after inoculation with starter cultures and liquid rennet. The soft curd is broken up and then cooked at 46-48°C, drained and pressed on perforated plates before being cut into pieces and transferred to the moulds where it will be pressed. Asiago Pressato has a mild, delicately milky, flavour. Like Asiago d'Allevo, the Pressato version enjoys DOP status.

Rennet: liquid, calf's
Outer rind: thin and springy
Body: white or slightly straw-white in colour, with deep, irregularly distributed eyes
Top and bottom: flat or almost flat, 30-36 cm in diameter
Height/weight: 11-15 cm / 11-15 kg
Territory of origin: the provinces of Vicenza and Trento, the hill country and low-lying area beneath to the west of the river Piave in the province of Treviso, and some municipalities in the province of Padua

Cansiglio

Produced all year round on the Cansiglio plateau, this proudly ancient cheese comes from pastures that lie over one thousand metres above sea level. Raw milk is used from Bruno Alpina cows nourished with fresh grass or hay dried in the mountains. It is heated to 38-40°C and coagulates in about 10 minutes. The soft curd is broken up into rice-sized granules and cooked again at 45°C for a further 10 minutes. Next, it is transferred into moulds, where it is pressed for a few hours and then salted in a brine bath. The cheese will be ready for table after spending a month in a cool (about 10°C), very damp room. Periodically, the rounds are turned over and, if necessary, scraped clean. If maturing goes on for more than six months, the cheeses are treated with linseed oil. Initially mild, Cansiglio's flavour acquires fullness and intensity with ageing.

Rennet: liquid, calf's
Outer rind: thin, soft and light-coloured
Body: even-textured with small, sparse eyes. Straw-white in colour
Top and bottom: flat, 30-35 cm in diameter
Height/weight: 7 cm / 6-7 kg
Territory of origin: the Cansiglio plateau in the province of Belluno

VENETO

291

Carnia

Carnia has been made at Padola for as long as anyone can remember. Today, part-pasteurised milk is used so a milk-based starter-culture is inoculated to encourage coagulation. The milk comes from Bruno Alpina cows. The soft curd is ready about half an hour later and is cut into rice-sized granules. It is semi-cooked at 42-43°C for about 10 minutes and then drained before being transferred to moulds for 48 hours. Next, it is salted in a brine bath. The rounds mature at about 12°C in a room kept at 60% humidity. Every week, they are turned over and once a fortnight, they are scraped. Carnia is mild and delicate on the palate when young, acquiring tangier notes when well matured.

Rennet: powder, calf's
Outer rind: robust and yellowish in colour
Body: round, close-packed eyes, Straw-yellow in colour
Top and bottom: flat, 30 cm in diameter
Height/weight: 8 cm / 6-6.5 kg
Territory of origin: Padola in the municipality of Comelico Superiore, in the province of Belluno

Casalina

Casalina is a characteristic cheese from the Marca Trevigiana area. In the past, it served to use up milk that had gone sour. Today Casalina, sometimes known as "Casalino", is made using pasteurised milk inoculated with a milk-based starter culture and liquid rennet. Coagulation takes only a few minutes and the soft curd is then broken up into hazelnut-sized lumps. After the whey has been drained off, the firm curd is semi-cooked at 45°C and transferred into hoops. The rounds are then dry-salted. Two days later, the Casalina is ready for consumption. It may also be matured for a few months in damp rooms at a low temperature. Since it is a relatively fresh cheese, it has no outer rind. The body is white, firm and fairly soft, becoming crumbly with maturing. On the palate, there is a dominant sourish note.

Rennet: liquid, calf's
Body: white, firm and soft, becoming crumbly with maturing.
Top and bottom: flat, 15 cm in diameter
Height/weight: 6 cm / 1 kg
Territory of origin: the province of Treviso

Casatella Trevigiana

The name of this cheese derives from the Latin *caseus*, or "cheese", although some prefer to think of it as coming from *casa* ("house") because it was once the typical cheese made at home. Whole milk, usually pasteurised, is coagulated at about 4°°C for 15-20 minutes. The curd is broken into large granules and then transferred into moulds for about a day. The hoops are removed and then the Casatella is salted in brine. On the second day, it is ready for the table but leaving it to mature for seven days will enhance its fragrance. Casatella has no outer rind. It has a creamy, buttery texture and a milk-white body whose mild flavour reveals a characteristic note of acidity that distinguishes Casatella from other similar products.

Rennet: liquid, calf's
Body: creamy with a buttery consistency. Milk-white in colour
Top and bottom: flat or slightly convex, 8-22 cm in diameter
Height/weight: 4-6 cm / 0.4-2.2 kg
Territory of origin: the province of Treviso and a few municipalities around Pordenone and on the Friulian plain

Comelico

Whole raw milk from Bruno Alpina cows is coagulated for about half an hour at 35-36°C. The soft curd is cut in two stages. The first reduces the pieces to half the size of a walnut, and the second to that of a grain of rice. The curd is then cooked at 45°C for 10 minutes. It is pressed for five or six minutes and put into hoops in a cool place for one day. Salting is also carried out in two stages. The rounds go into a brine bath for two days and are then dry-salted on top and bottom for 12 hours each. After 60 days, during which time the cheeses are scraped and turned over every other day, the cheese is ready for consumption. Comelico has a fairly mild flavour.

Rennet: liquid, calf's
Outer rind: soft, light brown in colour
Body: the body presents medium-sized, evenly distributed eyes. Pale straw-yellow in colour
Top and bottom: flat, 30 cm in diameter
Height/weight: 8 cm / 5 kg
Territory of origin: the municipality of Santo Stefano in Cadore, in the province of Belluno

Fodom

A new type of cheese created fifteen years ago, Fodom is named after the placed where it is produced. Part-skimmed milk from Bruno Alpina cows is coagulated at 36-37°C for 30 minutes. When the curd has formed, it is cut into granules the size of a grain of sweetcorn and then cooked at 45-46°C for 30 minutes. The whey is drained off and the curd transferred to hoops, where it is pressed mechanically. Pressing is carried out in two stages, first for 10 minutes and then for one hour. The cheeses are then salted in a brine bath for two days. The Fodom will be ready for the table after maturing for two months, during which time the rounds are turned over every other day and scraped once a month. Its flavour is fairly mild.

Rennet: liquid, calf's
Outer rind: hard and dry. Yellow in colour
Body: close packed medium to large eyes. Pale straw-yellow shading into brown with maturing
Top and bottom: flat, 30 cm in diameter
Height/weight: 8-10 cm / 5 kg
Territory of origin: the municipalit y of Livinallongo in the province of Belluno

Formaio Embriago or Ubriaco

This cheese has an ancient tradition, dating back to times when oil to treat the outer rind was scarce and expensive, forcing the cheesemaker to fall back on grape pomace and must. Obviously, it was made in the months that followed the vintage, from the end of September to early November. Curd is obtained by heating the milk at 33-35°C for about half an hour. It is then broken up into granules the size of a grain of rice and cooked for 15 minutes at 45-48°C. After the whey has been drained off, the curd is transferred to hoops. Next, it is salted, either in brine or using a mixed technique of dry-salting and brine baths. Twenty days later, the rounds are placed under fresh pomace from black grapes. The varieties used are Raboso, Cabernet and Merlot. They will stay there for about two days, and are continually sprinkled with wine from the press. After this, the cheese is ready for the table but it may also be matured for one or two months. Formaio Embriago has a richly aromatic, tangy and invitingly moreish flavour all of its own. Rounds of Montasio, Asiago d'Allevo or Latteria may also be "inebriated" in this way.

Rennet: powder, calf's
Outer rind: rather thick. Purplish or wine-red in colour
Body: firm and redolent of milk and wine. From white to straw-yellow in colour
Top and bottom: flat, 25-28 cm in diameter
Height/weight: 8 cm / about 5 kg
Territory of origin: the province of Treviso, on the left and right banks of the river Piave

Monte Veronese d'Allevo DOP

Low-fat Monte Veronese d'Allevo is the most ancient of the cheese types made by mountain cowherds. Until recently, it was produced exclusively in the mountain dairies of the Monti Lessini range. The current name is relatively recent but even when it was called Monte Vernengo or Grasso Monte, the terms used until the end of the nineteenth century, its characteristics and cheesemaking procedure were the same. It is a medium-fat, semi-cooked cheese made from Pezzata Nera cow's milk part-skimmed by allowing the cream to rise to the top. The milk is coagulated raw at 33-34°C. It takes about 20 minutes for the curd to form, after which it is broken into rice-sized granules and then cooked at 50°C for 10-15 minutes. After transfer into hoops, the curd is taken out and salted dry or in a brine bath. Ripening lasts for a minimum of 90 days, if the cheese is to be consumed at table, and for a minimum of 6 months (but may last as long as two years) if the product is for grating. The more mature version may also be enjoyed at table by those who prefer full-flavoured, tangily aromatic cheeses While they are maturing, the rounds are regularly turned over. The outer rind is hard, dry and fairly dark in colour. Inside, the body is firm and white, if made during the winter, or straw-yellow for summer Monte Veronese d'Allevo DOP. There are very few eyes, only slightly more than those found in the whole-milk cheese. On the palate, it is mild and fragrant, tending to acquire tanginess as maturing advances. The d'Allevo version of Monte Veronese can generally be found in dairies situated high up in the mountains. It is not unusual, especially in summer, to come across rounds made with milk from the high-altitude summer pastures.

Rennet: liquid or powder, calf's
Outer rind: hard, dry and fairly dark in colour
Body: firm and white, if made during the winter, straw-yellow in the summer version. There are few eyes, only a few more than in the whole-milk cheese
Top and bottom: flat or slightly convex, 25-35 cm in diameter
Height/weight: 6-10 cm / 6-9 kg
Territory of origin: the Monti Lessini range in the province of Verona
DOP status awarded on 1 July 1996, regulation no. 1263

The photograph illustrates three stages of maturing. The colour of the outer rind ranges from greenish straw-yellow to gold and pale brown.

Monte Veronese

Whole or full-fat milk Monte Veronese is a relatively recent cheese type which, like Monte Veronese d'Allevo, enjoys DOP status. Milk from Pezzata Nera herds is coagulated unpasteurised at 33-34°C. The curd forms in about 20 minutes and is then broken up into lumps the size of half a walnut. The soft curd is then cooked for 10-15 minutes at 43-46°C. Next, it is transferred to moulds and either dry-salted or immersed in a brine bath. The cheese matures in 30 days, during which time it is turned over regularly. Monte Veronese has a deliciously mild flavour.

Rennet: powder, calf's
Outer rind: thin and elastic. Pale to deep straw-white in colour.
Body: ivory-white or slightly straw-white in colour if made during the summer, with small, evenly distributed eyes
Top and bottom: flat or slightly convex, 25-35 cm in diameter
Height/weight: 7-11 cm / 7-10 kg
Territory of origin: the Monti Lessini range in the province of Verona

Morlacco

The name "Morlacco" comes from the inhabitants of Morlac-chia, the mountainous regions of Istria and Dalmatia, who in ancient times settled on the Grappa massif. Whole or part-skimmed milk is coagulated (raw in the mountain dairies, pasteurised elsewhere) at about 37°C for roughly half an hour. The curd is broken up into walnut or half walnut-sized pieces and may be cooked at 39°C, or simply kneaded, standing for a few minutes between sessions. After being left to stand for a suitable period, the curd is poured into plastic containers, which have replaced the wicker baskets that were once used. Salting may be dry or in brine, and is repeated over the course of several days. Monte Veronese takes about a fortnight to mature. It can be aged for up to two months. During maturing, the cheeses are washed with brine periodically. Morlacco has a rather salty flavour.

Rennet: liquid or powder, calf's
Outer rind: vestigial, lined and soft. Yellow or straw-yellow in colour
Body: white and soft. The eyes are small and very marked if the cheese was made with raw milk
Top and bottom: flat, 25-30 cm in diameter
Height/weight: 8-10 cm / 6-7 kg
Territory of origin: the zone at the foot of Monte Grappa and the Grappa massif

Cow's milk

Nostrano di Malga

This a very ancient type of cheese that once had an even lower fat content and was matured for longer. Today, it is made from June to September using milk from Bruno Alpina cows that have grazed on fresh grass. The raw milk is skimmed by allowing the cream to rise and usually inoculated with a small quantity of whole milk to obtain the fat content desired and prevent the cheese from becoming too dry. It is then coagulated at 32-40°C for 30-50 minutes and the curd is broken up into sweetcorn-sized pieces. The next stage is cooking at about 42-46°C, after which the curd is transferred into moulds and pressed for one day. Then comes salting, which may be either dry or in a brine bath. Nostrano di Malga matures in about 30 days, during which time the rounds are turned over and washed with brine. It has an intense, mild flavour that acquires tanginess after the fourth month of ageing.

Rennet: liquid or powder, calf's
Outer rind: hard and smooth. Pinkish yellow or brown in colour in the mature version
Body: firm, with small, evenly distributed and fairly close packed eyes. The colour varies from white to yellow
Top and bottom: flat, 20-30 cm in diameter
Height/weight: 7-12 cm / 2-7 kg
Territory of origin: the mountain and foothill areas of the province of Belluno

Pecorino Veneto

This limited-production cheese has its origins in the past when sheep farms were much more common. Ewe's milk, mostly from Massese sheep, is inoculated with calf's rennet as lamb's or kid's rennet are difficult to procure. Coagulation is carried out at 37°C and takes about 20 minutes. The curd is broken up into sweetcorn-sized granules and then cooked, if a hard cheese with a long shelf life is desired. Otherwise, it is transferred to moulds raw. The uncooked version yields a soft cheese that is ready for the table much sooner. Generally, the rounds are ripened at 36-38°C for a few hours. Pecorino Veneto has a characteristically mild flavour free of tanginess.

Rennet: liquid or powder, calf's
Outer rind: thin and fairly hard. Straw-yellow in colour
Body: firm, varying in colour from white to straw-white
Top and bottom: flat, 22 cm in diameter
Height/weight: 8 cm / 2-2.5 kg
Territory of origin: the provinces of Padua and Mantua, and the municipality of Anguillara in the province of Padua

Renaz

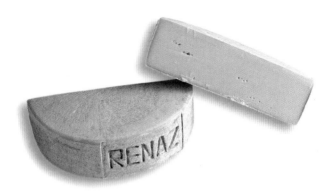

A new type of cheese created 15 years ago, Renaz is named after the placed where it is produced. Part whole, part skimmed raw milk is coagulated at 36°C. The process takes about 20 minutes. The curd is broken up into granules the size of half a grain of wheat and cooked at 46°C. It is then transferred to moulds and pressed in two stages, first for 10 minutes and then for about one hour. The rounds are then salted in a brine bath for two days. In the following three months, they will be regularly turned over, scraped and treated with linseed oil before finally going on sale. Renaz has a rather tangy flavour.

Rennet: powder, calf's
Outer rind: hard, yellow in colour
Body: Straw-yellow in colour, with sparse, medium-sized eyes.
Top and bottom: flat, 40 cm in diameter
Height/weight: 8 cm / about 5.5 kg
Territory of origin: the municipality of Livinallongo in the province of Belluno

Ricotta Affumicata

Whey from the milk of Bruno Alpina cows is heated to 90-100°C with added salt and vinegar. The coagulate rises to the surface, where it is collected and transferred to cloth sacks. The sacks are hung up to drain for a few hours, then their contents are pressed and dry-salted. The Ricotta takes one week to mature, during which time the cheeses are smoked over green conifer wood fires. Naturally, the product has no outer rind. If matured for at least one month, the body becomes hard and suitable for grating. Smoked Ricotta from Cansiglio, made in the area's mountain dairies, is particularly well-known. Citric acid is widely used as a fermenting agent and beechwood is popular for smoking. Ricotta Affumicata is ready to go on sale after one week.

Rennet: vinegar or citric acid
Body: soft and brown in colour, with a characteristic smoked flavour
Weight: about I kg
Territory of origin: the area of Agordo and Sappada in the province of Belluno, the Cansiglio flatlands and mountain diaries in general

Schiz

When fried fresh in butter with salt, this cheese *schizza*, or "spurts", drops of whey all over the hob, a characteristic that has earned it its name. In Alpago, it is also known as "Tosella". Very fresh, whole or skimmed, raw milk is coagulated at 35-36°C in 20-40 minutes. The curd is then broken up into sweet-corn-sized granules and, after being quickly drained, is transferred to moulds with a variety of shapes ranging from circular to rectangular. For the homemade version, a colander is often used. Schiz is eaten almost as soon as it is made. Salt is added at the table. The cheese has a milky aroma and very little flavour. Since it is unsalted, it tends to be insipid.

Rennet: liquid or powder, calf's
Body: soft, slightly grainy and whey-rich. White in colour
Top and bottom: flat
Height/weight: varying from 1-2 kg
Territory of origin: the province of Belluno, especially the area around Agordo

Index of cheeses